STOP Auto Repair Rip-off

Guide to Prevention and Maintenance

Mario Sasso and Michael Ross

Detselig Enterprises Ltd.

Calgary, Alberta, Canada

Canadian Cataloguing in Publication Data

Sasso, Mario, date
    Stop auto repair rip-off

ISBN 1-55059-094-4

1. Automobiles—Maintenance and repair.
2. Automobile repair fraud.   I. Ross, Michael, date
II. Title.
TL152.S27 1994   629.28'72   C95-910000-8

© 1995 Detselig Enterprises Ltd.
210-1220 Kensington Rd. N.W.
Calgary, Alberta, T2N 3P5

Detselig Enterprises Ltd. appreciates the financial
assistance received for its 1994 publishing program from the
Department of Canadian Heritage, Canada Council and the
Alberta Foundation for the Arts (a beneficiary of the Lottery
Fund of the Government of Alberta).

Cover design by Dean MacDonald

Printed in Canada   ISBN 1-55059-094-4   SAN 115-0324

Contents

Disclaimer

This book is not intended as a replacement for the services of a mechanic, but as a guide in choosing one and in identifying common repairs and maintenance procedures. While every effort has been made to ensure that the methods and recommendations in this book are sound and accurate, results will vary with each owner and auto shop. Neither the authors nor the publisher accept any legal responsibility nor any liability for the outcome of any repair, nor for any errors or omissions. The reader should always consult with a mechanic for all serious automotive problems.

Acknowledgements

We are very grateful to Barry Rust for providing us with this opportunity. His guidance and suggestions have greatly improved the original concept.

A special thanks to Linda Berry for doing such a fine job on the editing and design along with her co-workers.

We would also like to acknowledge Raymond Cheung for his efforts in the original design of the manuscript and all those at Detselig who contributed to the finished book.

We also appreciate all the teachers who introduced basic skills and knowledge about the automotive industry over the years.

Introduction

Up until 10 years ago, any car owner with some training was able to do basic repairs to a Ford Galaxy, Toyota Corolla, Honda Civic or Chevy Impala, with only a small selection of tools. To see someone working on a car on a warm afternoon nowadays is rare. Why? Because of the new technology entering the transportation industry daily. Vehicles have changed significantly since they were first introduced late in the 19th century. So much in fact, that a person almost needs a degree and an expensive assortment of electronic equipment to perform all of the necessary maintenance!

As well, not everyone who owns a vehicle wants to spend their day off working under a dirty hood, covered in grease, trying to repair their faulty engine. Those who do have some mechanical knowledge can save a substantial amount of money by doing their own basic repairs, but it is becoming almost impossible to effectively tune up a modern automobile to factory specifications. Today's vehicles are run by extensive computer systems and without technical training and expensive equipment, it is not practical to repair the complex problems they incur.

As the technological gap in car repair widens, car owners are beginning to leave the repairs to professionals. Today, everyone who owns a car will have to deal with an auto repair shop. Most of the people we have talked to have said this is not their favorite place! But when your car has broken down and you start work at 9 a.m. the next morning, it puts you at the receiving end of the mechanic's appraisal. Most of us have hectic schedules and little time to search around for an honest and competent shop.

In order to protect yourself as a consumer, you must learn how to deal with these shops. We have designed this book so that you can deal with any auto repair shop in the most effective and cost-conscious way.

By learning basic technical information, you are better prepared when you take your car in for repairs. It doesn't make sense to take a car to the shop for a tune-up when you don't know what they are going to replace and whether it *should* be replaced.

Is this scene familiar? You have left your car at the shop. Upon returning, the mechanic tells you that the car needs the front brake pads changed and, while they are at it, can they also rebuild the brake calipers as they are getting old? You know the brakes are squealing and likely need new pads, but the calipers?

Did you realize what was really needed or did you feel helpless and at their mercy? Were the brake calipers, in fact, perfectly fine?

Service salesmen can make the car owner afraid to drive away without having the recommended repairs done, all the while explaining how much cheaper it is if the work is done all together. In some circumstances this is true. For example, while changing the clutch, the shop could also easily replace a worn bearing in the transmission at a nominal cost. However, if they are replacing a few bearings in the transmission, they don't necessarily need to change the clutch, which is significantly more expensive. This manoeuvre is quite common with unsuspecting car owners.

How many times has the repair bill been more than you expected? Are you often unsure if a bill is fair, yet have little or no choice but to pay it? Do you understand what your mechanic is telling you? When it comes to your safety on the road and your paycheque, it's time to take these concerns seriously.

Have you ever felt like a sitting duck for every mechanic or garage owner who wishes to take an expensive vacation? Well, don't be a duck anymore! Before you wander into the next repair shop, arm yourself by reading this book and learning how to protect yourself. It is filled with invaluable information that will give you the upper hand when dealing with that mechanic.

With the average maintenance repair at over $100 and the average major repair at over $400, getting a vehicle repaired can be a major expense. However, owning and caring for your vehicle can be a pleasant, sensible and even enjoyable experience. All you need to do is make your vehicle more of a priority and less of a mystery. So, we do not go into great depth about the intricate parts comprising an automobile; instead we explain the more important and common repairs and leave the greater detail to the myriad auto repair books available.

We reveal valuable insights and information about the car repair industry that will not only save you hundreds of dollars in a single repair job, but also reduce the stress and aggravation involved in the process. Step by step, we guide you through basic maintenance requirements that help you avoid the repair shop in the first place. You need no previous knowledge of cars to apply this information effectively.

We teach you how to avoid costly car maintenance by exposing fraudulent situations, by explaining what a car does and does not need and by guiding you in choosing the most appropriate garage for service. Each section of this book gives detailed information on maintenance, repair and scam prevention techniques for every major part of a car. Each section can be referenced as required, but we recommend you read the book through to obtain an overall understanding. Later you can brush up on a specific chapter just before you go out to have that car part looked at. So sit back, grab a highlighter pen and read on!

Section One

Types of Garages

Before You Choose a Garage

There are typically five different types of garages to choose from: 1) large chain specialty, 2) gas station service bays, 3) independents, 4) large chain general repair, 5) new car dealerships. Each type has its advantages and, of course, its disadvantages. The important thing is to consider what type of garage to which to bring your troubled car. Once that is established, finding a competent mechanic is much easier.

Before entering a shop, be able to identify with some conviction where a noise (or leak, etc.) is coming from in your car, when it happens and any noticeable odors. The more clearly you can describe the car's symptoms, the better the mechanic will be able to discern where the problem lies. This alone will save you considerable amount of money off the labor portion of the bill.

When you describe it, avoid telling the mechanic what you think the problem is. If you start by saying that the car needs a new water pump and the timing adjusted before they fix the valve clearances, you are putting yourself in an unfavorable position, because they won't accept responsibility if these repairs don't fix the problem. This is not the way to deal with a mechanic, or any professional for that matter. Imagine going to a doctor and telling him what you think the diagnosis is and what prescription you need to cure it. How would he feel about having an untrained person treading in his area of expertise?

For example, you might think that a noise is coming from the tire, when in fact it is coming from the brakes. No one knows for sure without inspection. When you take your car to the tire shop, they may also suggest replacing the tires to alleviate the problem and could justify this by pointing to the worn tires. Now, because you went in with a preconceived notion, and the mechanic agreed, you have set yourself up.

How? The mechanic will either try and sell you whatever service the car needs or *that which you think the car needs*. If you agree that it's the tires, then they will change the tires. The brakes are the real problem, but you just spent $400 on a new set of all-season radials and the car still can't stop! Consequently, you need to spend more time and money to fix the malfunctioning brakes.

The best procedure to follow when you are unsure of the problem is to take your car to a few different repair garages. By getting an opinion from three or four of them, you will be able to distinguish where the problem is, how severe it is and how it should be repaired. With that information, you can now go to the appropriate shop to obtain a proper repair at a reasonable cost, after first calling around for the best quotes.

Never panic when you go to a garage. *You drove in*, so don't forget, you can usually drive out again without something awful happening. Almost everyone is doing a free inspection these days and you don't need to feel obligated or pressured to get the work done right away at this particular shop. Take advantage of detailed estimates from as many shops as is convenient for you.

It is in the shop's best interest to explain the estimate properly if they want you as a customer. It is important that you make sure that all parts and labor are detailed clearly. If they are not, the shop can take certain liberties in the final amount of the bill and you don't want that miscellaneous charge to be more than what was written down.

A good trick is to ask the mechanic if any other work needs to be done while they still think you are going to authorize everything right on the spot. A "chiseller" might go for the extra charge and then not want to put it down in writing on the estimate when you tell him you are leaving. If the mechanic refuses to put down anything in writing, you are probably looking at a large rat, with you holding the cheese. Don't give him any, just leave.

It is not a good sign if a shop doesn't want to give you a copy of a detailed written estimate. Find one that will. Usually there are several shops in a given area for comparison shopping. You will be amazed at the range of both prices and problems quoted by shopping around – often up to a difference of 50 percent. Contradictions are not only due to fraud, but also differences of opinion and, in many cases, incompetence. Think of your car as a person and your mechanic as a doctor. It never hurts to get a second opinion. Always be sure to leave on good terms, saying that you must consult with someone about the work and may be back. This allows you to compare all information from other shops and make an informed decision. (If you have a friend who is knowledgeable about cars, this will be a great time to call and discuss what you have been told.) It also prevents you from blowing up and closing the door on what may be the most honest and reasonable mechanic in town, just because it sounds expensive. Later, you may find other shops agree with the original diagnosis and want to charge even more.

Be extra careful of garages that have only been in business for a short time. Some really dishonest shops will set up somewhere, make their money and then move shop to the next unsuspecting district. With the potential of making lots of money at each place, they are easily motivated to continue this procedure. It can be somewhat of a dice roll with a new shop, since there are no old customers around to talk to. If the shop is an honest one bent on creating a good reputation, it may supply the best service and prices anywhere with great enthusiasm. It pays to meet the person who owns the new shop: his or her personality may be an indication of the quality of service and honesty. A garage that has been at the same location or expanded their facilities nearby, and has a steady flow of old customers, is the best sign you can find for a garage. The disadvantage is that they may not be able to take your business because they are so busy. That's okay, just book ahead for an appointment.

Another method of finding a good shop is to ask someone who needs a lot of car repairs.

Ask limo and taxi drivers, pizza deliverers, firefighters, police officers, ambulance drivers or anyone with company cars. Another source is to ask an insurance company which garage it uses to get estimates. But remember, just because the garage is good to its big customers doesn't mean it will

15

treat you the same. Therefore, try and draw a strong association between yourself and the reference you give. If possible, get a friend to come down and introduce you to the owner.

A fancy-schmancy high overhead shop on a busy corner in the most expensive part of town may have to charge more to meet expenses. They also may feel less dependent on word-of-mouth due to drive-by business and go for the big score every time they smell a sucker. A higher price doesn't necessarily translate into better work. Often price and quality are not related. Prices for the same work can vary dramatically.

Often, after dealing with a shop for some time, a relationship develops. Don't be lulled into a false sense of security. (Just think of our political system if you need your caution recharged.) The main advantage of having a friendly relationship with the owner is so that he knows you as a nice, happy, regular customer worthy of getting good service and prices. And, if a problem arises, you have someone to speak to. The other thing you definitely don't want to forget is the detailed written repair estimate listing parts needed, labor and all miscellaneous charges.

Some jobs may require an initial inspection. In this case, find out the cost to check it and get it written down. If you then decide to go ahead, try to make the inspection price part of the repair bill.

Always get a good warranty on the work you are getting done and read the large and fine print. Warranties may read differently than what you understood from the mechanic.

Signs in some major franchise shops state that no warranty work will be done unless all other problems found are also fixed at the same time at the owner's expense. In this case, the warranty may be used by an unscrupulous shop to lure customers back, possibly by installing second-rate parts that are sure to fail quickly.

The rest of this section helps you understand which venue is most appropriate for the different types of repairs your car needs. It is up to you to know which type of garage you need, since the first mechanic you see will most likely want your business, if they have the basic equipment necessary. The first garage may not be the garage you want to fix your car, so take the job to the appropriate professional.

Large Chain Specialty Repair

These are the well-known shops that seem to be on every major street. They usually specialize in one or two types of repairs, most often brakes, muffler, transmission or lubrication.

If you know what the specific problem is, and *if* the shop is an honest one, they have the capacity to do a good job at a reasonable price. The mechanics have extensive experience with their specialty and the company can get good deals on parts due to high-volume purchasing. Another advantage is that they are usually fast and convenient, parts are in stock and you don't need an appointment.

These shops have huge advertising budgets and are usually in high-traffic locations. This means they are constantly getting in a flow of new customers (like you). They may not have to depend on word-of-mouth from happy customers, or repeat business, which means your satisfaction is less important. Be careful, as their loyalty is not to you. Some of these shops will try and use the dreaded "Bait and Switch" (B&S) on you. B&S is when they advertise a low price on a "package deal" to get you in the garage and then convince you to buy a whole lot of expensive parts and services you don't need.

Have you gone into one of these shops to get the $69 front brake package and left with a repair bill for $369 that included a complete brake job? It happens to many car owners, so don't feel bad. For example, a shop may convince someone that the car brakes are badly worn. Once the owner is so frightened that they are scared to drive the car, the shop is almost guaranteed that the owner will sign the authorization form. Remember, *don't panic* when you are at a garage.

Gas Station (Service Bays)

If you frequent a privately-owned station and have developed a rapport with the owner, this may be a good choice for basic repairs: routine oil changes, changing the fan and alternator belts, and tuning up an older car. Many gas stations today are equipping their repair facilities to be able to perform other types of services. Some of them now provide diagnostic tune-ups, air conditioner reconditioning, brake repairs and tire services. Deal only with reputable companies to ensure quality service. Otherwise this can be a dangerous place for the unsuspecting car owner.

Distinguishing between reputable companies and not-so-reputable ones is not easy. The first and best choice is word of mouth. When you hear about a service bay that over-charged a friend or performed unsatisfactory work on their car, are you likely to have them fix your car? A good reference is just as important.

Check if the company you are dealing with is approved by an Automobile Association. Individual automotive centres can apply for approval from their local AA, who will inspect the facilities to ensure that equipment is up to their standards and that the mechanics are qualified. Approved shops may have stickers displayed from various AAs. The key is to check the year for which the sticker is valid. Being certified does not mean the shop is honest, but it at least indicates they should be able to do a good job if they wish.

Many regular maintenance jobs are done at a gas station when filling up, because it's convenient. A prime example of this is getting the oil checked. Since this is done every time you fill up with gas at a full service station, the odds of a problem occurring increase. While most gas station attendants are honest, there are exceptions. The attendant can look under the hood and say you need oil, showing you a partly dipped oil dipstick. (A dipstick is a metering device used to measure the level of oil in your car. See your owner's manual to locate it.) At this point the attendant pretends to add oil with an empty oil can and then gives you a full dipstick reading. You end up paying for a can of oil you didn't need. (By reading the oil and lube section of this book you can easily avert this sort of thing.) It is also a good idea to check and make sure that the right amount of gas has been added. You can do this by looking at the meter on the pump; if not the attendant may underfill the tank and pocket the extra money.

Occasionally, a careless attendant cleaning the front windshield will damage the windshield wiper, possibly ruining it. If this happens and you drive away without noticing, the station will likely deny any responsibility at a later date. When you catch the problem right away, usually the station will replace the broken wiper on the spot. (Most service stations have windshield wipers in stock.)

The problem of a broken windshield wiper is minor compared to what can happen to an unsuspecting motorist travelling long stretches of highway. An unscrupulous station mechanic on a deserted strip can sabotage your car so it no longer runs, then charge you to fix the damage, without you being able to prove anything against him. This is a multi-million a year industry and they know full well that when you are in their station, it is likely you will get any problem fixed there, rather than having the car towed some distance.

Since it is unwise to let a mechanic at a shop in the middle of a highway even check the tire pressure without watching carefully, do not let him tackle any computer-related or high-tech repairs without the proper equipment and training. This equipment is very expensive and requires a considerable amount of training to be able to read the manuals that go along with them. You will have no one to complain to if something does go amuck. Even when the mechanic starts out with the best intentions, if he makes a mistake and blows a $1 000 computer in your car, he may not be willing to admit and pay for it. The problem is now yours and you will end up paying for his mistakes. It is best to stick with very basic repairs at gas stations if you have a modern car.

If you are travelling a deserted highway and find you need gas, make sure you do everything yourself. Put in the gas, check your own oil and fluids. If you let the attendant do it, at the very least get out and watch carefully. Always watch anyone doing anything to your car whenever possible. They will be less likely to try and put one over on you. Remember: they don't know how much or how little you know unless you tell them!

If you still aren't convinced of the dangers faced when travelling that lonely highway, here's one more story. Some Happy Travellers are driving along on their trip when they decide to pull over to Big Jesse's garage to fill up the gas tank. Big bad Jesse says, "Howdy, it would be my pleasure to fill'er up. Would you like the oil and tires checked?" The Happy Travellers say, "Sure!" and go on chatting among themselves. Well, Jesse checks the oil, no problem. Then he checks the tires, again no problem – until he punctures a hole in the side of one of them. Jesse takes their money for the gas and tells them how unfortunate it is, but one of the rear tires looks a little low. Then he takes off the tire to patch it, saying it will only cost a few dollars and take a few minutes. The Happy Travellers are still happy and suspect nothing. Now their car is up on the lift with the tire off. A few minutes later, Jesse tells the now Less Happy Travellers that while fixing the tire he noticed that their brakes were dangerously in need of repair. The owner of the car tries to explain that he had his brakes done only six months ago. However, Jesse persists and says they did a poor job, and hey, the life of the whole Happy Family is at stake here. Eventually, Jesse wins out and the little stop at the gas station ended up costing the now Unhappy Travelers over $400. Not a bad profit for a tank of gas since Jesse didn't really fix the brakes. Most would agree that this is a high price to pay someone for checking the air in the tires.

Since it is getting harder and harder to find a full service station these days, it is better to learn the basics and get into the habit of doing these simple things yourself. If you are really opposed to touching your car, a simple solution is get out of the car and watch the person doing the maintenance checks. If you feel unsafe getting out at a gas station, either because it is deserted, or the area is suspect, get the gas and leave. Check other things somewhere else. The Maintenance and Repairs section explains the basics of checking fluid levels. Watching a service attendant do it once at a busy and reputable gas station will clarify things even more. If you know what to watch for, you will be able to tell quite easily if something suspicious is being done to your car.

Independents

Independent garages are there for the sole purpose of fixing cars. They don't receive revenue from new car sales or high volume muffler or tire sales. They also are not backed by a huge corporation. Fixing cars is what they do and it is how they make their money. Therefore they can be really good and honest, or really bad and dishonest, depending on the personality, values, skill and financial situation of the owner.

Ask friends if they have someone they are really happy with and use their name when you go. References are very valuable when choosing an independent garage.

When you go to an independent, look around the garage and see if there is any highly technical equipment; it will stand out. If not, make sure the garage doesn't do any complex repairs on your late model car. Also check if there is a mix of newer luxury cars along with older or economy cars in for service. A shop may be great at fixing a '67 Chevy, but will not have a clue about how to fix some parts on a new Cadillac. If you take a modern car to an incompetent garage for what seems to be an electrical or engine problem and they accidentally damage an expensive component, they will never admit it and you will end up paying for it. Due to lack of good diagnostic equipment and know-how, they may also replace good parts unnecessarily in random fashion until the car works again.

So, for modern complex problems it may be wise to go to the dealer or a well-known and highly-recommended independent garage. Even then, unless you inspect a mechanic's credentials, you really don't know how up to date he is, no matter where he is working. Modern cars are changing so quickly it is hard for anyone to keep up. Locate a shop with an owner on site who you get along with and who takes the time to talk to you. Get to know him and build a relationship. Let him know that if he does right by you, he can expect you to be a loyal customer and also spread the word for him. In return, let him know you want great service at a fair price.

Large Chain General Repair

These large shops will usually try and fix almost anything that may go wrong with a car. Quite often they specialize in selling tires or are affiliated with a department store. This gives the garage instant name recognition and brings in customers. In addition, these shops usually have huge operating and advertising budgets. One thing is for certain, there you will never meet the owner. There is an advantage to this situation when you have a problem with the service you receive: a long chain of command that you can keep moving along until someone gives you a fair shake.

These shops are image conscious and don't want to be caught red-handed in a scandalous situation. This is not to say that you are any safer from being taken advantage of. They will usually try and make you happy so they can get back to business without you causing any problems for them.

It is good strategy to try and solve a problem with management when the shop is busy and full of potential customers. The smart shop will not want to lose new customers by arguing with you.

For example, if you go to Ed's garage and have a problem with Ed, who can you go to, Ed's mother? You are left with court options and filing better business bureau reports against Ed, who has been there before. A big chain shop may give in to a persistent customer who has a valid complaint just to avoid the negative publicity. Often these shops will have separate customer complaint divisions to deal with any problems that arise.

If Ed is honest and a good mechanic, then he will give you good service and get to know your car. In contrast, the counter person you deal with at a chain general repair shop is often not even a mechanic, but a salesperson, who may come and go with time. This set-up gives you little contact, if any, with the mechanic working on your car. This means that the information the mechanic gives to the salesperson may change by the time it gets to you. For example, the mechanic may discover that a part on your car needs a minor adjustment, but the salesperson tells you it must be replaced right away in order to increase the bill.

It is common at big shops to use a flatrate system. This means that the price of a particular repair job is set according to a predetermined amount listed in a book at the shop. The flatrate estimates the amount of time the repair should take and that number is multiplied by the shop's hourly rate. We have mixed opinions about this system. In one way it is good because a mechanic can not purposefully drag out a job and charge for unnecessary time. But when the job goes quicker than expected, you still pay for the scheduled time. This could be a benefit because it should steer the shop away from hiring poor mechanics who take too much time to complete a job. The main drawback could be when a mechanic rushes and does poor work so that he can finish ahead of time but still get paid for the additional time allotted to the job. In a sense, the mechanic is then getting paid for two jobs at the same time in a busy shop where he has another job waiting.

Often a part of the bill goes to the mechanic, so he has incentive to work faster than he should. The key to getting a fair shake with the flatrate system is to make sure that you are only charged for work that is really needed. Once you know what the problem is, it is easy to compare prices among other shops with a flat rate. Decide on a fixed amount of time for a job before it is begun, to provide incentive to the mechanic to finish the job in a reasonable amount of time and to avoid overbilling. When dealing with a flatrate shop, don't feel gouged when the job takes a little less time than the hours you are charged for. However, when the time is substantially less, for example 50 percent, you need to question what has transpired.

Big chain shops are always offering special low-priced services aimed at getting customers into the garage. Often these "deals" are very good, but be careful not to get talked into unnecessary work. Because these shops do such a wide range of repair work, specials serve to bring in many new customers. An honest shop will look for work that genuinely needs to be done; a dishonest shop may encourage work that is really optional, or possibly not needed at all. If you go in for a low-cost special and a shop tries to pressure you into work you previously had not considered, get a written estimate and then a second opinion. Remember, just because the car is up on their hoist for an oil change doesn't mean you are committed to having a total brake job.

Any shop by itself in a high traffic location should be watched carefully. A steady flow of new blood makes them less reliant on word-of-mouth and repeat business than an out-of-the-way shop. Also, if the shop has no apparent competition, prices may be higher and scams easier, as you are not as likely to go down the street for a second opinion. On the other hand, a shop that is out of the way and starving for business can sometimes be even worse. For example, if the owner's rent is due, he may try and make you pay for it! Ideally, you want a slightly out-of-the-way shop that is busy and has competition close by. Another thing to watch for is that the shop is filled with independent motorists like yourself and not just used-car business repairs or other large contract work. The presence of a lot of cars with similar company logos, the same make of car or a number of cars with commercial plates may indicate the shop does a lot of contract work. The presence of both is fine, but contract-only work means your satisfaction may be insignificant to the owner.

Dealer Garages (New Car)

Dealer garages are found attached to almost any new car dealership for most makes and models of automobiles. This type of garage specializes in repairing the same make of car they sell. If you are a valued customer who is always buying new cars from the dealership and once in a while you bring in an older car for out-of-warranty service, it is in their best interest not to upset you. If you are lucky enough to be in this position, a dealer garage may be for you. Still, don't assume that just because a dealer handles a top-line car that you will get top work done. A dealer may sell the most expensive cars and still have a terrible service department.

It is no secret that dealer garages are usually much more expensive than other shops. They justify higher rates by saying they use only genuine factory parts and pay their mechanics more. The dealer's overhead is huge and when car sales are slumping the money has to come from somewhere – make sure that your name isn't "somewhere."

Another concern with dealer garages is that they often have a steady flow of business because of new car maintenance and warranty work, thus making you less important in the big picture, unless they see you as a potential car buyer. A little trick to improve your standing at a dealer garage is to get the manager to take a look at your car for trade-in value before having it serviced. This not only puts you in the category of a potential customer, but also gives you someone else to talk to if you have a problem.

As with big chain general garages, you may have to deal with a counter person who is pretending to be a mechanic. This person is often just a smooth-talking salesperson who may be making a commission on all the extra parts and labor they can talk you into. You don't normally meet the mechanic. Sometimes talking to the mechanic can help clarify the problem to him, and make the repair quicker and easier for everyone.

The main advantage of a dealer garage is that if you have a high-tech car with a complex problem, the mechanics are experienced with the type of car they specialize in. What may seem like an obscure problem to other shops may be quite routine for them. The mechanics will be up to date on the latest diagnostics and will likely know about strange recurrent problems your specific model is prone to. However, all this expertise and expense is often wasted on simple mechanical problems and oil changes.

Just as in any other type of repair facility, there are both honest and dishonest dealer garages. If you are considering using one of these shops, try and talk to people who have had their cars serviced at the shop in question to see what experiences they had. It is also a good idea to look around the shop when you get there. If the car is an older model, take a look around for other older cars being serviced; if there are none, this may not be a good sign. Do not confuse cars from the dealership's own used car lot (older cars with temporary or no licence plates on them) for other customers like yourself. If all the cars in the service area are newer and of the same make they sell, the shop may prefer to do mostly warranty work and will likely not care much about satisfying you. A mix of various years and makes of cars is a good sign. Remember that the owners of cars under warranty have no choice but to have the car serviced at the dealer; they do not prove regular customer satisfaction.

Finally, when choosing any type of shop, simply look at the garage and notice if it is organized. Check to see the working conditions of the mechanics: are they favorable and comfortable, or too hot or cold? Do the mechanics seem happy or miserable? Mechanics are people, and will respond to better conditions. An uncomfortable and unhappy mechanic is less likely to take care and pride in his work. Also, it is unlikely that the best mechanics would choose to work in the worst environments. It takes training and ongoing upgrading to be a top mechanic and they are in high demand. Realistically, though, you are judging a garage and not a fine art museum. Do not expect the garage to look as clean as a kitchen.

Section Two

Maintenance and Repairs

Tune-Ups

Many of us look after our cars incompletely. We polish the hood until it resembles a mirror, buy new mag wheels, new stereo systems and air fresheners, but when the car starts making squeaks, rattles and chirps, we hope that the annoying sounds will go away on their own. If your car lacks power to climb a speed bump, or takes a few attempts to start the engine or stalls every morning, then it probably needs a tune-up.

Dry starting – when your car doesn't start easily – is harmful to the engine. The lubricating system in the engine normally takes a few seconds to begin working. If it takes several minutes in the morning to cold start the engine, it may get damaged. This could also lead to premature wear of the starter motor, an expensive part.

As these symptoms develop, they require immediate attention or the condition will get worse. Have the ignition system tended to about every 5 000 km, more under severe driving conditions, or as the manual states. Rather than wait for a mechanic to tell you the air filter needs to be changed or that there is no transmission fluid, learn to look after these vital basics yourself. Read your owner's manual to check the service intervals and follow suggestions in this book.

Remember to have your car serviced more frequently for regular city driving, which by the way is considered severe service. Due to the additional wear caused by stopping and starting frequently, filters, fluids and spark plugs need to be changed more often. Some symptoms of a neglected car include: rough idling, engine run-on, backfiring, an expensive gas bill, black smoke coming from the exhaust, constant stalling and lack of engine power/response.

Repair shops have their own ideas of what it means to tune up a car. This makes it difficult for the car owner to price a tune-up, because they rarely know what they are paying for. Many shops only change the **spark plugs** and **air filter** and **adjust the timing.** This basic service is what most shops mean when they advertise a "tune-up special."

However, even this simple job needs clarification. It is important to ensure that good quality spark plugs are used to replace the old ones. Ask about the selection of brand names. When it comes to replacing the air filter, it is not difficult to tell when a new one is needed. The air filter is located inside a big round device resembling a cake pan under the hood. By loosening the twist screw in the middle and removing the top you will see the air filter. The air filter is shaped like a ring; the filtering material can easily be seen on the sides of the ring and this should not be all black and dirty. Often a mechanic will blow some pressurized air onto it to remove the surface dust. You should be able to see light pass through the filter. Even though the air filter is not very expensive, you don't want to be convinced to replace one that is still clean. Remind the mechanic to check the air filter to prevent any future problems with the car.

Modern cars, when running smoothly, require less servicing than their old counterparts. This is due in part to the addition of computers and microchips and it is to your advantage to have a **computerized diagnostic tune-up.** Since most late-model cars are highly computerized, this method will give you the best performance analysis. It is sufficient in most cases to do the basic tune-up mentioned, plus change the **gas filters, distributor cap** and **rotor** if they need replacement. Replacement of the distributor cap and rotor will make the tune-up more expensive, but they will not need changing every time. It is best to go to a shop familiar with your make and year of car.

The typical older car needs a different tune-up than the newer self-adjusting computerized vehicle. Older models require somewhat more labor when doing a proper tune-up, which should include everything the modern car requires plus adjusting the spark plugs, and **exchanging the points** and **condenser** (if you have them). Unlike the more modern car, older cars require no expensive diagnostic equipment to make adjustments, which can all be done with a few simple tools.

Regardless of how old a car is, a good shop should quickly check these additional areas: **belts** and **hoses**, the **alternator**, the **cooling system, spark plug wires, ignition wiring PCV valve** and **emission control devices**. It is unlikely that you will remember all of these items, so make a list and give it to the mechanic. There should not be an extra charge for checking these things, but replacing them will of course cost extra.

A good tune-up should return the gas mileage to normal, restore power and ensure proper exhaust emissions. Unless there is a mysterious problem, a good mechanic can tell what areas need to be looked at.

Do not have the car tuned up on a road trip unless absolutely necessary. Have it done before you leave on the trip. People traveling out of town are attractive and vulnerable targets for dishonest shops.

Keeping your car well tuned is another important step in caring for it. Your car has the potential to last more than two decades if it's looked after properly and is not a lemon to begin with. Find a good mechanic and develop a reliable relationship. Make time in your schedule to check your car.

Engine Diagnostics

If you are having starting problems, or any other mysterious engine problems for that matter, go around to a few shops and see if someone can figure it out in the initial look-over. Sometimes you will get lucky and a mechanic will recognize your problem and solve it easily. Your car may have a loose battery cable that was overlooked and will cost nothing if caught.

When you find yourself getting a varied response to the nature of the problem and expensive quotes, go to a high-tech shop with good engine diagnostic capabilities. They will look up the factory specifications for your make and model and then determine specifically what is wrong. Whether it is a misfiring spark plug or lack of engine compression, the mechanic should be able to find out. A shop with top notch engine diagnostic equipment and technicians will be more expensive, but still cheaper than unnecessary repairs.

Today's high-tech cars have "black boxes" to operate many parts in the car. These mini-computers require sophisticated equipment, which some of the smaller shops don't have, even though they do great work otherwise. The boxes run the computerized fuel injection system, ignition, temperature control and many other systems in the car. These pieces of electrical equipment cannot be fixed with a wrench. Having the right equipment is important and time saving.

A diagnostic engine analysis of a computerized car gives the mechanic detailed information about its engine. These machines are quite sophisticated and expensive. They require competent technicians to operate them and interpret the data. We have encountered a number of repair shops that couldn't figure out what the report said.

Getting competent engine diagnostics at a reasonable price is no easy task. Normally there is a charge as soon as they hook up the car to a diagnostic machine. It is important to find out what the initial charge is and how much an hour after. Believe it or not, most shops still charge you the same regardless of whether or not they find the problem.

Set a firm cash limit for solving the problem *in writing* when you fill out the work authorization. Make it clear that if they do not find the problem by the time you have spent the specified amount, you will go somewhere else for the repair.

If you don't, an incompetent shop could literally work on your car for days and charge you a fortune. Worse, a crooked shop can let the car sit in the garage without doing anything and still charge you for hundreds of dollars in diagnostic testing time.

Setting a limit gives them incentive to find the problem within the specified time and then profit from the repair job itself. It is hard to say what a reasonable amount of time is to find a problem because some are trickier than others. For most problems the limit would be two hours of diagnostic time. The down side of this is no matter how long it takes, they may charge you the two hours.

You should receive computerized reports on the car's performance when you get a diagnostic test done on the car. Keep this as it not only proves that the tests were performed, but also gives valuable information to a future mechanic if the problem resurfaces.

Transmission

The transmission is another one of those integral parts of your car that you simply cannot do without. The wheels of the car would not turn when you step on the gas without the transmission. Obviously, transmission shops may be inclined to exploit this fact. In most, if not all shops, as soon as they hoist up the car and open up the transmission to look at it, there is a substantial charge. This makes it expensive to shop around. The transmission is complex and not every garage will attempt to repair it – the bulk of this work is done by specialty shops. The complexity and expense of transmission work makes it a perfect tool for a garage to rip you off. It is not uncommon for an unscrupulous mechanic to turn a minor $80 repair into one worth hundreds of dollars, or even into a total transmission overhaul.

When you approach a shop, make it clear from the start you are looking only to find the minor problem with the transmission and to have it repaired at a reasonable price. Hopefully, you will be "twice lucky" and only a minor repair at a nominal cost will be required and the mechanic you have chosen will tell you the truth. For the average person, transmission repairs will not be reasonable unless you are knowledgeable about the transmission.

This chapter shows you how to keep out of the transmission repair shop by preventive maintenance, avoiding scams and proper care. Once in a shop for a complex transmission problem, you are essentially at the mercy of the mechanic's skill and honesty. When the bill is going to be high, about the only thing you can do is forfeit the initial inspection fee and try going somewhere else, hoping the diagnosis and cost of repair will be lower. If you know someone who has a vast knowledge about cars, this would be a good time to use a favor!

For those of you who drive an older vehicle, chances are someday transmission work will be needed, if you plan on keeping the car. Prepare for the worst by calling around to reputable shops and getting quotes on replacement of the transmission on your particular car before you have a serious problem. Be sure to ask for a complete price, including all parts and labor. Also determine if they will install a new or rebuilt transmission and what their warranty is. By doing this before you have a problem, you will be able to assess the cost differences between shops and the value of the transmission. Don't wait to do this right before you are going into a shop, or they may recognize you as the person who called. An unscrupulous shop will try to sell you a new transmission, even if the problem requires only a $10 repair, thinking you are ready for it. However, if the mechanic is telling you the truth and the transmission is truly shot or ready to go anytime, you may find that when you approach another shop for the repair, the cost may come very close to putting in a new one. If the car is older, it may make more sense to have it done and get a good solid warranty, rather than have another expensive problem a few months down the road.

If you have an automatic transmission, one of the most overlooked steps to keeping the transmission trouble-free is to attend to the transmission fluid. It is a good idea to check this fluid whenever you check the oil. The proper way to check the transmission fluid follows: turn on the car. Be sure to park on a level surface. It is also a good idea to shift slowly through all the gears and then back to park. Turn off the motor before checking the transmission fluid. You can check the fluid easily at this point by pulling out the transmission fluid dipstick (similar to the one for oil).

Aside from checking the level, be sure that the fluid has not changed color. If the fluid takes on a dark brown tinge in color or smells like it is burnt, the fluid needs to be changed. The exception to this is Dextron II transmission fluid which will sometimes turn a little brown but should never take on a burnt smell. Just to confuse things a little more, the biggest and most noticeable exception are the synthetic transmission fluids that will turn very dark and even smell burnt. However, you should only be using one type of transmission fluid in your car, the one stated in the manual, so you only need learn the characteristics of one type.

When the fluid begins to show characteristics of breakdown, it is wise to have the fluid and filter changed immediately. If the fluid appears okay, but is a little low, it can be topped up.

Be careful not to overfill the fluid as this can actually cause damage to the transmission.

If the fluid is constantly running low, it is sign of a problem because little fluid should be lost over time – it is likely you have a leak. Anti-leak agents can be bought at automotive supply stores; these are often helpful in sealing small leaks.

The transmission fluid and filter should be changed completely when it is worn, which is anywhere from 40 000 to 64 000 km, again depending upon driving conditions. This service is not expensive and can greatly increase the life of the transmission. The trick is not to get suckered in for unneeded work while you are getting this service performed. Make it clear from the start that the transmission is running fine and all that you want is a fluid and filter change, maybe a few minor adjustments if needed and absolutely nothing else, no matter what. It is also important to make sure the mechanic puts the correct type of transmission fluid back inside your car.

There are two types of automatic transmission fluid, Type F and Type G. Putting the wrong type in a transmission not only leads to poor performance, but may also damage some transmissions. Know what type you need before going to the shop, by checking either the manual or with your manufacturer. Then insist on that type. Listen to what the mechanic tells you about your transmission fluid. If no information is offered simply ask them what the color looked like. Most mechanics will be happy to tell you what they think, and because they are aware you are not in the market for further work, their analysis of the transmission may be more truthful.

It often helps to simply say that you have no money for additional repairs at this time. A transmission shop does not stay in business by charging some of those ridiculously low basic service specials often advertised. These specials are lures to bring in a large volume of cars off the street that will hopefully lead to more expensive repair bills.

It is not unheard-of for shops that specialize in cheaper jobs like oil and lube to form a liaison or even share ownership with higher-priced specialty shops. Sometimes the oil and lube shop will be used to steer customers over to the transmission shop. This works well because a high volume of people will pull in spontaneously for a $25 oil and lube, but not many for an unneeded transmission repair. The oil and lube shop acts as the bait which sets you up for the kill.

An example of this scam may go like this. You are driving along in your perfectly running car and suddenly you see a sign advertising a real cheap oil and lube job. You decide that the car deserves it, pull a U-turn and drive into the service bay. You hop out of the car and let them do their thing. Soon the manager, with a concerned look on his face, calls you over to show you that there are metal shavings on the oil pan plug. He says this means you are in desperate need of a transmission overhaul. He may try and get you to do it at his shop if he does this kind of work. More often, he will act as though he has nothing to gain and suggest you go to another shop he highly recommends. Usually you will be given a business card and a coupon to further direct you to the shop he recommends. The mechanic finishes the oil and lube and sends you on your way, reminding you how urgently you need tranny work and to go to the shop he recommends immediately.

Once you leave he calls his buddy at the transmission shop to tell him your plate number and the song and dance you got. Often, simply presenting the coupon is all the transmission shop needs to know what is going on. Then his friend can give the identical second opinion you are looking for to be sure that the work is needed. The next day, the manager of the oil and lube shop also reminds his buddy to pay him the $200 referral fee if you take the bait and wind up getting $1 000 in unnecessary transmission repairs. (By the way, a small amount of metal shavings in the oil pan is normal.)

Another variation of the same scam is for the shop to send you over for a simple transmission fluid change with a great coupon and lots of kind words about the quality of the shop. Once you are at the transmission shop and your car is apart, they begin to work on you, building up a case to convince you that substantial transmission work is required in the near future. They will further point out that since they have the transmission apart, it will be cheaper and better in the long run to let them do the work right away. It is easy to get pulled into a scam like this, forgetting that the transmission was working perfectly fine an hour ago.

The problem lies in that the oil and lube shop may be telling you the truth and you may, for example, need a fluid change. The only way to know is if you check your own fluid regularly and know what it is supposed to look like. Just as there are dishonest shops, many are honest and just because someone is giving you bad news, doesn't make him or her a liar. Always get a second unrelated opinion in these cases and know your fluid.

By now it is obvious you should avoid being talked into expensive transmission repairs when the car is running fine. What about when you actually do have a transmission problem and need to have it serviced? Aside, that is, from taking a lie detector kit into the transmission shop with you and hooking it up to the mechanic, or going to school and becoming a transmission technician.

The best strategy is to always try and steer the mechanic towards finding an inexpensive and simple solution to the problem. This means you have to keep a positive, relaxed attitude and not make any hasty decisions. (There is really no way for the average person to know if what the mechanic is telling them about the transmission is true other than how well the transmission was working before you came to the shop.) Many transmission problems, both major and minor, appear to the average customer to have the same outward symptoms and so a crooked shop can distort the facts.

For example, Jerry is driving along in a hurry, but to his sorrow his car seems to have lost its passing gear. Well, off goes Jerry to a local transmission shop to find the problem. After Jerry describes the symptoms, the mechanic tells him there is a minimum $40 charge for trying to find the cause. Jerry hesitantly agrees and the car is put up on the hoist. Many transmission shops have this minimum charge; one of its main functions is to keep the customer in the shop for the repair, making it expensive for them to shop around for opinions. The mechanic spends some time working on the transmission and then comes over to Jerry and says, "It doesn't look good, I think a total overhaul would be best. We have a special on for only $800." Jerry tells the mechanic that a friend of his, who is also a mechanic, said it could be a problem with a cable in the transmission that would need only minor adjustments. Even though this is true, the mechanic talks Jerry into the expensive repair. Of course, Jerry has no way of knowing the truth and eventually agrees.

The approach taken by Jerry would have worked fine if the mechanic was competent and honest and the repair should have only cost about $50. Jerry might have fared a little better if he had taken a different approach.

Approach two might have gone like this. When he pulled into the transmission shop and was told about the initial $40 charge for diagnosis, he said, "I am not interested in spending much more than that to fix the car. I'm planning on selling it anyways." After describing the symptoms to the mechanic, Jerry asked him what the odds were that the problem was a simple one and could be fixed for a relatively small amount of money. Note that Jerry still had not committed to the $40 charge and therefore could leave at any time. Plus, the mechanic sensed that Jerry would not likely go for an expensive repair.

If the mechanic suddenly seems to change attitude and lose interest in the job, then it is a sign to Jerry that he is only after the big score. If the mechanic seems helpful and concerned, even after Jerry makes it clear that he will not go for a big repair bill, Jerry may choose to go for the work and see what happens. If the mechanic takes the transmission apart, then finds a simple problem, it makes sense to have it fixed for a reasonable price in addition to the $40 service charge, since they are already into the job. However, if the transmission does need a major overhaul, the mechanic's word will more likely be true because they don't expect you to get the work done at their shop, and so have nothing to gain. In fact, the mechanic actually has more to gain by finding a simpler solution to the problem. The mechanic must be convinced you will not go for an expensive repair.

Another option for Jerry is to take a drive around to a few other transmission repair shops before deciding on which shop to use, again describing the problem, finding out what their minimum charge is and feeling them out. He can always return to the shop he thinks is the best bet. On top of this, Jerry will have learned more about what the problem might be and will appear more knowledgeable when talking to the mechanic he chooses.

Since going into some transmission shops is treacherous, it makes sense to take care of the transmission to prevent the whole scene from ever occurring. Aside from avoiding unneeded work and maintaining good transmission fluid, there are a number of other things that can be done to prevent problems from occurring. Remember, a little prevention can go a long way in saving future aggravation and expense.

If you are hauling a trailer or towing some other heavy object, have a transmission cooler installed. The cost is not that high, about $100, and it is well worth it in the problems it can save. Another tip is to properly maintain the radiator; if the radiator doesn't function well, it can damage the transmission and cost more than if you had just serviced the radiator to begin with.

A simple but little known tip to enhance the life of your transmission is, when cold starting the car, let it warm up until it is idling normally before shifting out of park. Never shift between drive and reverse unless the car is completely stopped. Also, when stopping to park on a hill, always apply the emergency brake before you release the regular brake. This will prevent the car from bearing its full weight down on the transmission gears and possibly damaging them. This practice should apply to all hills, no matter how slight, as the car is heavy and this sort of wear can quickly add up. Don't spin the wheels on slick or loose surfaces because when the tires finally catch, an unusually high tension will be put on the transmission that can lead to damage.

Take good care of the transmission and it should last a very long time. Proper maintenance and care is without a doubt the best defense against costly repairs.

Batteries

The car battery is a storage battery, as it supplies electrical current when the engine is not running. It differs from the flashlight batteries in that it can be completely recharged while the engine is operating.

Today's high-tech computerized cars drain the battery even when the car is turned off. Therefore, if you leave your car parked for a long time (more than one month) it likely won't start when you return. Don't panic if this happens; it just needs a boost to recharge it (read the steps on jump starting on the next page).

Complete drainage of the battery can be prevented if you disconnect it before you leave your car for long periods of time.

Most of the batteries being used today, in fact for the last 10 years, are **maintenance-free**. This means the storage cells are sealed at the factory. This way, the sealed battery doesn't lose as much solution (**electrolyte**) as conventional batteries and typically lasts longer without any maintenance. You can check the **charge indicator** on top of the battery to see if it is still good. Each manufacturer uses a different system that can be identified by reading the instructions on top. Or, have a mechanic check it periodically to ensure that a strong charge is always present.

Batteries are made of cells which contain about 2 volts of electricity each; since cars operate on a 12 volt system the battery should have 6 individual cells. The battery will have two **terminals**, one positive and one negative, marked with a "+" and "−" sign respectively. The positive terminal is slightly larger than the negative one. The cable leading from the terminal to the frame of the car is the negative cable. This *grounds* the car's electrical system and prevents it from short circuiting. The other cable is the positive one, which supplies the charge to the engine operating system. The positive terminal is normally made of a heavier gauge wire and has a number of other wire attachments for different car systems.

Batteries are sold with a specific guaranteed level of charge. Some are rated at a minimum of 36 months, others can last up to 72 months (6-year battery).

If the battery fails before its allotted time, you are entitled to a refund based on the number of months that it fell short, so keep your receipts and the warranty into the glove box in case you need them.

A mechanic uses a **hydrometer** to measure the amount of electrolyte in the battery. This is a hand-held device that tells the mechanic how strong the solution inside the battery is. A **load tester** is also used to determine whether the battery can supply the correct amount of charge when the demands on your car are high. If the battery is dead, the mechanic should charge it up and then perform this test. This test can be the difference between replacing or recharging the battery. It is simple to change a battery and there is usually no charge for installation, but the battery itself can be expensive.

Common Causes of Premature Battery Failure:

1. Alternator not charging the battery — The alternator is not functioning properly and even if you replace the battery it will drain the new one.

2. Corrosion on terminals — This causes a weak contact point for electricity. Clean it off with a solution of baking soda and water and re-attach.

3. Low water level	The level of electrolytic solution in the battery is insufficient to maintain a proper charge for your car. Keep this topped up. Maintenance-free batteries don't require this.
4. Too old	Self explanatory.
5. Dirty battery cables	Clean with cable cleaners.
6. Loose alternator belt	This will affect the performance of the alternator, so get it tightened by a mechanic.
7. Bad battery	Replace existing battery.

Caution! Be careful of fluid leaking out of a damaged battery, it may be sulfuric acid and can be very dangerous. Besides burning the skin, the acid gives off hydrogen gas, so avoid smoking or open flames nearby, as it can cause an explosion.

How to Boost a Battery

When someone is stuck with a dead battery, it is nice of you to help them, but it is important that you do it properly. Make a note of the proper procedures for giving another car a boost or "jump start," so that it will be handy when you need it. Only connect batteries of the same voltage to prevent alternator damage, and when positioning your car, avoid touching bumpers with the other vehicle. Switch off all accessories in the dead car.

Caution! Boosting someone else's battery can damage the **alternator** (an important and expensive part in the charging system).

Leave the engine off when "jump starting" another car to protect your alternator. If their car doesn't start within a few attempts, disconnect and start your engine or you may kill your own battery. You must decide how much risk to take to jump their car by leaving your car running during the boost. An occasional jump start in your car's life will not hurt it, just don't make it a habit. The alternative is to call an automobile association and have them hook up their charger (if this service is available).

Hook up the cables in the following order:

1. Red cable clamps onto positive terminal of dead battery.

2. Red cable clamps onto positive terminal of good battery.

3. Black cable clamps onto negative terminal of good battery.

4. Black cable clamps onto the grounded metal part of the dead car. Many people will just hook onto the negative terminal, but this can be dangerous: there may be hydrogen gas hovering over the battery and any sparks from the connection will easily ignite the gases.

Caution! keep all clamps free and clear of each other to avoid sparks and injury.

5. After letting the battery charge for 30 seconds or 1 minute, depending upon the age of the battery and the extent of the drainage, start the car with the dead battery. If it doesn't start, check the cables, wiggle the wires a bit to ensure a good connection and try again.

6. Disconnect cables in the following order, steps 4–3–2–1.

Most batteries are made by a few big companies and sold under different private labels. It is important to replace the battery with one of the right size, since each car is different. A retailer will have a listing to help you find the right size and type of battery for your car. Then it is up to you to decide what quality of battery you want. Your main considerations should be the credibility of the place you are buying the battery from, the warranty provided and then price. Remember, price is not necessarily related to quality. Buying a battery from a big name company with an "as long as you own the car" warranty is not a bad idea. It is usually more expensive, but if the battery dies you can bring it in for a free replacement (read the warranty to make sure this is the case).

The down side to a lifetime warranty is that you will have to wait for the battery to begin to die in order to get it replaced. If you live in a cold climate, this may leave you stranded someday because batteries lose efficiency and are pushed harder in cold weather. The other option is to buy a good quality battery on sale and replace it about every four years. Never buy a battery from an auto dealer: they are normally 25-30 percent more expensive than your local parts store. Also, take the old battery to the recycling depot or check if the place you bought it from will take it in to recycle it.

Cooling System

The cooling system is responsible for removing the hot temperatures produced from the moving parts and burning gases inside the engine. There, temperatures can get high enough to quickly break down metals and cause the engine to seize without an effective cooling system. Overheating automobiles occur as frequently as flat tires and running out of gas. If your car has a temperature gauge and it passes the red mark, prepare to pull over.

The cooling system contains **coolant** or **antifreeze** (the green liquid that protects the engine). Without it your car would overheat during the hot season and freeze in the colder climates. Most mechanics recommend changing it completely every two years, since it loses its protective ability over time. You must be careful with antifreeze, as it is a toxic chemical, so do not let your pets or children touch or lick it up if any spills on the floor while topping up the radiator.

The word **coolant** refers to the mixture of antifreeze and water in the **radiator**. It is important to have the correct ratio of anti-freeze to water in order to get the best protection for the engine. The climate in which you live determines the ratio of coolant required – something a mechanic will know. If the coolant was all water, it would freeze during a cold winter in Winnipeg, and had you been driving to California during the summer, the coolant would probably boil away soon after you departed for your great adventure. That is why you need antifreeze. Antifreeze raises the boiling point and lowers the freezing point of water. This is what allows a car to be driven in the coldest temperatures without freezing and in hotter climates without evaporating.

To maintain a healthy cooling system, check the radiator for cracks, tearing or corrosion – these are early signs of wear and might be easily sealed before you need to rebuild or recore the radiator. If you do alot of highway driving or love to travel, make it a habit to check the front of the radiator for insects, leaves and other unwanted pests. After driving on the highways for long periods these can build up and affect the radiator's cooling ability. The cool air that hits the front of your vehicle while driving cools the engine coolant which in turn cools down the engine. It's a continual process of cool fluid taking away internal heat and then moving to an area where it can be cooled, so that it can go back to do it again. With this in mind it is a good idea to regularly spray the front of the radiator with water. This will keep bugs out of the radiator.

If your radiator shop tells you that you need a new radiator and can't provide a reasonable explanation other than a small leak, it can often be quickly repaired by sealing it. Small radiator leaks can be sealed by a radiator repair shop. All they do is solder the opening shut. Some companies claim that by pouring their product into your radiator, any leaks will be sealed automatically. We have no experience with this and little evidence to prove otherwise. Also, we have found that a professional job doesn't cost very much.

The most common major problem with the radiator is a ruined core. Usually this is caused by time and gradual deterioration, often sped along by poor fluid maintenance. When this happens to the radiator, it is possible to have it "recored" or reconditioned instead of buying a new one. This is usually sufficient and much less expensive. An important thing to do is to keep the cooling system free of rust and corrosion. This clogs the vital passages inside, thereby restricting the flow of engine coolant. Mechanics can clean out clogged systems if they are not too rusted. They do this by "flushing out" the system. This will clean out and unclog any buildup present. Don't just drain, but flush also. If you don't get the system flushed, alot of old antifreeze remains in the system and will mix with the new. Since old antifreeze loses its rust prevention ability and effectiveness over time, this will reduce the quality of the coolant inside. A car owner can flush out a radiator by inserting a flush tube into one of the cooling system hoses. If you want to do this, please make sure you have the right hose, as people have mistakenly cut the wrong one. We believe that flushing out the radiator is best left to professionals for safety reasons. Proper maintenance will avoid costly overheating and repairs.

As an owner you can check the following:

1. The front of radiator for bugs and things
2. Proper fan belt tension (apply pressure on the middle of the belt with your thumb. A belt that dips about one half inch and feels fairly taut is usually good enough. To learn how they should look and feel, check them yourself right after they have been professionally adjusted.)
3. Cracked or swelling hoses
4. Coolant level

Caution! Never open the radiator cap while the engine is hot. Be aware that pressure has built up in the cooling system after driving. If you open the cap at this point it would be like opening up a can of shaken soda pop, and the boiling liquid could seriously burn you.)

---

5. Check also for any green leaks or puddles underneath your car.

Caution! That little fan under the hood automatically turns on when the temperature gets too hot in the engine. This also cools the engine coolant. On older cars this fan is attached to the engine and is on continuously, but on newer cars it won't turn on until the operating temperature in your car reaches a certain level. So when poking around under the hood while the engine is running, be careful of this fan as it may start suddenly and chop off your fingers. In addition, when the fan is running it is difficult to see due to its speed.

Maintenance check by a mechanic:

1. Thermostat
2. Pressure test
3. Fan belt

4. Level of protection available from the coolant (test liquid)

When you need the cooling system serviced, compare the relative cost to service ratios to get the best value for your money. In other words, when there is a small leak in the radiator, don't replace the whole unit, have it sealed or soldered closed. Use a shop familiar with radiator service. If a mechanic doesn't know how to flush the car's cooling system, the water pump could be damaged, which will likely be added to the bill (for newer cars it can be expensive).

Gasoline

Many people give little if any thought to what type of gasoline they put into their car, mistakenly thinking all are equal. There are many differences between gasolines which may have a positive or negative effect on a car's life and performance. The first and easiest step is to check the car manual or with the manufacturer to find out what quality or grade of gasoline is suggested for your car. Once you have decided what grade of gas to buy, you must then tackle the more difficult task of deciding from whom and where to buy it. Think of gasoline as drinking water to a car. Water is water, but obviously there are differences between spring water, water from a rusty tap, purified bottled water and contaminated water in an underdeveloped country. Similarly, differences in gasoline depend on how they are stored, the additives they contain and how they are refined. These differences can affect a car's performance just as much as the quality of water you drink can affect yours.

If you have ever heard someone complain that they filled up with a tank of bad gasoline, it is quite possible they were right. It does happen. Usually someone who knows their car well will pick up on this right away, noticing the car's poorer performance immediately after filling up. An unfortunate situation arises when someone not so in tune with their car doesn't realize that the gas is the problem and starts trying to find another reason for the car's poor performance. This can cost you unnecessary time and money trying to diagnose and fix a nonexistent mechanical problem with your car. The point is that if your car is well tuned and running fine before you fill up at a gas station, and then suddenly begins to run poorly, it is likely not just a coincidence; the chances are the gas is causing the problem.

Not all brands of gasoline are created equal. From the initial refining process on, there can be big differences between different brand names. Some gasoline is distilled in such a way as to be more volatile than others. To make things simple, think of every batch of gas as having two different parts, one more volatile and the other less volatile. The higher the percentage of the gas that is more volatile, the better for your car. It is important to understand this concept for several reasons.

The more volatile the gasoline, the easier and faster the car will start and warm up completely. This alone can greatly reduce the amount of engine wear on the car over the years. Keep note of how well your car starts and warms up when trying a number of brands of gasoline, as there are differences.

It is also important to understand this volatility factor in order to see why gasolines *with the same octane rating* can still perform differently. **Octane** is the ability of a specific gasoline to prevent **engine knock**, which is bad for the engine. The higher the octane number, the more it prevents engine knock and the smoother the engine will run. Higher performance engines or cars with many miles on them need higher octane fuels to function smoothly. This is important – an engine that doesn't run properly because of a low fuel octane level can eventually develop real problems.

Another sign of poor octane levels, besides a knocking engine, is when the engine continues to run and sputter after it is turned off. If your car is running roughly, try using the best premium fuel available with the highest octane rating, if you haven't been doing so already. It may solve the problem.

The trick then becomes deciding which fuel is the best. One method may be to ask someone, who drives a car similar to yours with no problems, which fuel they use and from which station. Then to give it a try. If not, it may take trial and error to find the best fuel. Part of the problem is that octane numbers listed at the pump don't give the whole story.

The octane rating that you see displayed at the gas pump is actually an average of the octane rating for the most volatile and least volatile parts of the gas. Therefore, two different brands of gasoline could both have octane ratings of 90, but may achieve them differently. Example: gasoline A – most volatile part octane equals 95. Less volatile part octane equals 85. Average: 90 octane at the pump. Gas B: most volatile part is only 90. Less volatile part is also 90. Average: a pump octane of 90. Gas A will perform better because it is the more volatile octane that your car reacts to the most.

In other words, just because two gasoline brands have the same octane rating at the pump does not mean your car will run the same on both of them. Unfortunately, the missing information required to make a better decision is not listed at the pump, and the task of trying to find the best gas for your car is basically left for you to test, while keeping a close eye on your car's performance.

When you are testing different types of gasoline, try and make sure the tank is near empty before trying the new brand to be able to make a clear and fair assessment. This way the last tank of gasoline won't mix with the new one to give you a false impression of what is really happening.

Unless you are testing different brands of gasoline, try and always keep the tank as full as possible. This helps prevent condensation from building up in the gas tank and causing all sorts of problems. Too much condensation will create water droplets in the gas and water is the last thing you want in the gas tank.

Another reason for keeping the tank full is that, as the gas level approaches empty, the fuel pump may start to suck up pieces of dirt, sediment or even water that settles at the bottom of the tank and move them through the engine where they can cause problems.

It is also a good idea not to overfill the gas tank. Fill it to the full line and no further. Overfilling can eventually lead to the creation of leaks in the gas tank.

Several alcohol-blended gasolines have popped up on the market. These are gasolines mixed with either ethanol or methanol. Methanol has been said to have a negative effect on certain parts of the car while ethanol blends have enjoyed better acceptance. All sorts of problems have been linked to the use of alcohol mixtures in gasoline by the car manufacturers, leading an informed motorist to think twice about using them. Profit margins are increased, without the knowledge of customers, by adding a mix to gasoline. It is difficult for consumers to protect themselves against this. The only yardstick is performance.

There are alcohol testing kits (used by establishments that sell alcoholic beverages) that one can purchase through restaurant supply houses. This may be worthwhile when deciding on a brand of gas that you intend to stick with. If the test proves negative, it is one less thing to worry about. The hardest part is finding someone local who sells the inexpensive and simple test kit.

Odds are you won't run into leaded fuel anywhere these days, as almost all fuels at the pump now are unleaded. However, if somehow you do find some of this outdated gas, it is not advisable to put it in an "unleaded only" car. For one thing it will destroy the catalytic converter, along with botching up your engine. The amount of money you save by using leaded over unleaded will come back to haunt you with more expensive repairs.

If you should happen to see one of those big tanker trucks filling up a station's huge underground gas tank, avoid purchasing gas there for a time. Similar to your car's near empty gas tank, all sorts of junk from the bottom could be stirred up in their holding tank, which may end up in your car. Realize that any gas you buy comes from a huge underground gas tank. Therefore, notice how busy and popular the station is. This may be a clue as to how long the gas may have been sitting in that tank. Gas at a busy station is less likely to be old, or tainted with water or sediment.

Always try and fill up at an established gas station. One woman filled up at a "no name" gas station and then had a great deal of car trouble. When she went to see a mechanic, the problem couldn't be found until finally the gas tank was drained. He was surprised to find a 70/30 mixture of gas and water. If you find yourself in this position, you may have to find a garage that can drain the bad gas for you.

Caution! Do not try to drain your own gas tank, it is very, very dangerous.

The other point is that you will have nowhere to dispose of the polluted gasoline in an environmentally-friendly way.

Another little tip is to not fill up when it is extremely windy and dusty or raining very hard. This will prevent unwanted water or dirt from finding it's way into the gas tank and polluting it.

If you must fill up under these conditions, be careful not to leave the gas tank entry port uncovered any longer than absolutely necessary.

These days, mainstream gasoline contains a number of additives that clean the engine, protect it and prevent rust. This means that if you use a good-quality gasoline there is likely little need for purchasing additional fuel additives. All of the fuel additives that a car needs should already be in the gasoline.

Every time you fill up the car you must remove the fuel cap. If this cap is lost or stolen it is important to replace it as soon as possible. Aside from preventing the gas from spilling or evaporating away, it also keeps dirt and water out of the fuel supply. The gas cap also has vents that allow air to enter the gas tank as fuel is consumed by your car. Your car may not run properly if the gas cap vents become plugged up. Gas caps also are needed to pressurize the fuel system to help it function better.

It is a wise idea to replace the gas cap at least every five years or so.

If the need arises, locking gas caps can be purchased to prevent someone from stealing the cap, siphoning gas or even putting a contaminant in the gas tank that will mess up your car. Aside from the above reasons, it is also unsafe for you to drive around without a gas cap – and also bad for the environment. Gas fumes are highly flammable and if ignited, the flame will travel into your gas tank and blow up your car. In addition, your gas will also evaporate into the air without a gas cap.

Now that you are striving for the best fuel for your car, it is just as important to regularly change the **fuel filter.** No matter how good a fuel you use, there will still be some dirt and other contaminants mixed in with it which must be cleaned out. The fuel filter, when working properly, will clean the fuel to a standard acceptable by the engine. These filters are especially important to cars with fuel injectors, keeping them from becoming clogged. You should have the fuel filter changed at least once a year (or sooner if recommended by your manual). Filters on fuel-injected cars are not changed very often because of the expense. It costs up to $100 just to remove and replace the filter because of its location. If you buy an older fuel-injected import car with problems that you've traced to the fuel system, first change the gasoline, then the filter and you should notice a dramatic improvement.

If you feel you have gotten a bad tank of gas, it may be wise to change the fuel filter sooner, just to be on the safe side. If a fuel filter becomes plugged with dirt, it will cause your car to lose power and, in extreme cases, cause your car to stall right out due to a lack of fuel. Fuel filters are usually simple and cheap to replace and it is well worth the while for the protection of the engine.

These days there are full-service stations everywhere. Regardless of whether it is intentional or not, mistakes do happen, as do outright scams. When an attendant is filling up your car, make sure to look at the pump. There are several reasons for this. One, to be sure that the correct grade of gasoline you have requested is put in; two, to be sure you get as much gas as you are paying for – often these stations are quite busy and an attendant is taking care of several cars at a time. He can get confused or not understand your instructions.

A third possibility is the attendant may wish to pocket a few extra dollars. This is most likely to happen when you are paying cash. The attendant will, for example, take $20 from you and only put in $15 worth of gas, hoping you don't notice. If you are paying for gas by credit card, keep the receipts to be sure you are not over- or double-charged on the monthly bill. It is also wise to tear up any credit card carbons because these can be used by an unscrupulous attendant to rip you off – the carbon records your card number and a copy of your signature. Make sure the attendant remembers to replace the gas cap, as sometimes they forget and leave them on top of your car. (More frauds are listed under the section on Gas Stations.)

Oil And Lubrication

The engine oil performs many important functions that are vital to your car's life span. The oil lubricates and protects the internal mechanical parts of a car and also helps keep the engine running cool. Today's oil has many special additives mixed in with it. These serve to clean the engine or prevent rust. The bottom line is that without oil, your engine will be destroyed, and with poor or depleted oil, it will be slowly damaged, leading to expensive repairs. With something this important, you would think there would be a big flashing sign telling you it's time to change the oil and what type of oil to put in. Since this option has not yet hit the market, it is important to be able to decide when and what type of oil change your car will require.

As oil is used in your car it gradually picks up dirt and other particles that pollute it. The additives in the oil also get broken down and used up to the point that they are ineffective over time. The speed with which this happens depends on a number of variables. Many automobile manuals give two different oil change intervals, one for regular driving and the other for hard or severe driving conditions. It is almost always wise to go with the shorter interval to be safe. If you live in a city, chances are you mostly take short trips, stopping and starting frequently along the way. Driving for only short distances with lots of stops on the way can be hard on a car, especially in cold weather where the car doesn't get to warm up completely. This type of driving is much harder on a car than long steady highway driving. If you drive like this, as most city people do, and want to be on the safe side, change the oil and filter about every two months. It may cost a bit more, but you won't have to worry about damaging your car by driving on bad oil.

There are other factors that also contribute to ruining the oil more quickly, conditions that put more strain on the engine than normal. Examples of these are driving in extremely hot weather, pulling a trailer or another car, or even loading the car down with heavy goods. Driving up mountains or in traffic jams can also wear down the oil. Another problem can be dust in the air. If you often drive down dirt roads kicking up dust, or are even just exposed to alot of dust in the air, it will have a negative effect on the oil. These type of conditions call for more frequent oil changes. Think of it as a shower for the inside of your car after some extra hard work. Remember it is always better to change the oil too soon rather than too late.

Engine oil comes in various **viscosities** (weights or thicknesses) from 5 all the way to 80. The higher the number, the thicker the oil is. The weight of oil needed depends on the seasonal temperatures and the driving conditions. Thinner oils are used in colder weather, while thicker oils are used in hotter weather. Today, motor oils have special additives that change the viscosity to suit a wider range of climatic and driving conditions, and can be used year-round in some milder climates. These multi-weight oils range from 5W20 to 20W50. These different combinations are available to better suit different situations and temperature fluctuations. The owner's manual will tell you which type and grade of oil to use for your car, but it is wise to contact a local dealer or mechanic to double check what best suits your particular local climate, season and use.

Everyone should know how to check their own oil level. It is very simple and should be done every time you put gas in the car. The only tricky part is to find out where the oil **dipstick** is located on your car. Simply watch a service station attendant check the oil to find out where it is (this service is provided free at full service gas stations). The car should be turned off and parked on a level surface to get a proper reading. Allow the car to sit for a moment to let all the oil settle into the oil pan. Then pull out the dipstick, wipe it off, replace it completely and remove it once more. This time check to see the oil level. Do this by referring to the bottom of the dipstick where there are two different marks: the top mark reads full and the bottom mark reads add. The oil level should never be above the full mark or below the add mark. It is best for your car to keep the oil level just below the full mark line. Have a gas station attendant add some oil to your car if it is a little low; there is only a charge for the oil. Be sure to check that he has not overfilled the oil level by performing the dipstick test again. If this happens, some of the oil must be drained. This is messier and more difficult than adding oil so be careful to avoid this problem. Add a little, check, add a little more, and so on, especially when doing it yourself.

Much of the wear and tear on a car can be avoided by regularly checking to make sure that the oil level is at the right height. When you add fresh oil to your car you are also freshening up the old oil a little, giving it some added effectiveness until the time you decide to change it completely. When adding more oil to your car, don't spill any on the engine. This can cause smoke when driving. It is best to wipe it up when this happens.

The difference between add and full is one quart of oil. If you are driving around on the add line you are missing a significant amount of oil. This makes the oil you do have work much harder and less effective at doing its required functions. This problem can be magnified in smaller cars that only take about three to four quarts of oil to begin with.

Warning: Many cars have a warning light that will flash if the oil level or pressure drops below an acceptable level. When you cold start your car, this light will briefly come on, which is normal. However, if this light comes on while driving it is best to stop and turn the car off immediately. Get out and check the oil; if it is really low add some (keep a spare quart or so in the trunk). If the light goes out when you try and start the car, head directly to a garage. If not, quickly turn your car off again and have it towed to a garage. Driving the car with too low of an oil pressure can destroy an engine beyond repair. If you're lucky the problem will be only a faulty oil pressure indicator light. Regardless, it is not worth the chance of blowing the engine.

It is also important to understand that this warning light will only go on when the problem is severe. Do not think that because the light is not on the oil must be okay. The light is only a last minute warning before disaster strikes.

Finally, the big question, when to cough up the $25 or $30 and have the oil and filter changed. These days oil and lube shops are everywhere. They are fast and should do a good job if you know what you want. Usually all the extras are yours for the asking at no extra charge. You know what type of oil you want, but when do you go? There is no hard and fast rule other than when the oil and filter in your car needs to be changed, it should be, or else your car will suffer. It is better to have an oil change too soon than to have one too late. On the other hand you don't want to waste a lot of money on excessively frequent oil changes.

Now that you are convinced how important it is to change the oil, let's change it. Make sure your car is good and warmed up before you head over to the oil and lube shop. Go at an off-peak hour and usually you can drive right in for a quick oil change. If the oil in your car is hot it will easily drain out of your car. When it is cold, some muck will likely remain in your car's system and get mixed in with the fresh oil. These days it is hard to see what most oil change shops are doing, because they work underneath the car from an excavated work area. It is worthwhile to ask the mechanic to please be sure to drain out all the oil. Sometimes if they are rushed, they will leave some old oil in the car. It also doesn't hurt to let them know you are watching what they are doing.

Before the mechanic puts oil in your car, make sure it is a brand and quality that you are satisfied with. If the shop uses a bulk tank to dispense the oil, it is up to you whether to trust them or not. Also be sure that a top-quality oil filter is used. This is a must because it prevents dirt particles which become suspended in the oil from damaging the engine. You don't want to be given a poor quality filter even if it is a little cheaper. Be sure that the filter is changed every time you change the oil. Not only is the old filter filled with dirty oil that will mix in with the new, but if it isn't functioning well or even clogged up, you can get real problems that don't justify saving the few extra dollars it would cost to replace it.

So now you have new oil and a new filter and you are ready to drive off, right? Well hold on, because you are still entitled to more. As a free service, the shop should **lubricate** a multitude of points under your car with a special grease to further prevent wear and tear on your car. They should also check all of your car's other fluid levels. If they need to be filled, there will be a small charge for the fluid used. The following fluids should all be checked in addition to the oil: **power steering fluid, transmission fluid, brake fluid, wiper fluid** and **engine coolant**. This is also a perfect opportunity to learn how to check these on your own. Before leaving the shop check your own oil level to make sure it is not over or under filled.

It is unlikely that your car will need any special additives or services that a shop may try to sell you. Everything a car needs should already be in a good quality oil. There are mixed opinions on these different solutions, but when getting a standard oil change under normal circumstances, there is really no need for them.

With the information presented in this section, an oil and lube job should be a worry- and trouble-free experience. If one uses a reputable quick lube shop, the whole procedure will take about 15 minutes with no complications. The price of the complete oil and lube is often listed right up on the wall of the shop, changing slightly with the different qualities of oil available. The problem arises when a garage claims to have found another problem that requires repair during a routine inspection. It is up to you to decide how much weight to give this. It is best to be most careful of the mechanic who reports a problem and also wishes to fix it for an additional charge. An uninvolved second opinion will be very useful in a case like this. The most credibility should be given to a shop that reports a problem that they neither fix nor recommend you go somewhere in particular to get repaired. This type of shop has nothing to gain from their advice other than stating what they believe to be true.

Exhaust System

As the serious problem of air pollution continues to worsen, car manufacturers have been required to find ways to reduce unwanted emissions flowing out of our cars. This has been accomplished by adding a number of different emission filters and devices. The most prevalent of the pollutants are hydrocarbons (HC), nitrogen oxide (NO) and carbon monoxide (CO). It is of vital importance – not only to you but also to the environment – that the exhaust system be in good working order at all times. It is the exhaust system which carries toxic fumes away from the car, filtering and neutralizing the most lethal gases before releasing the remaining gas into the air. To understand the importance of the exhaust system, it is necessary to realize from what it is protecting you. During normal operation, the car produces the deadly gas carbon monoxide which is odorless, tasteless and colorless. There are sometimes other gases that accompany CO, which have a smell detectable when walking behind a parked car. Unfortunately, these gases can be hard to detect when leaking slowly into the car along with carbon monoxide, which dulls your senses.

Caution! If you ever do detect the slightest exhaust smell in your car, immediately ventilate the car by opening the window. Carbon monoxide tends to sneak up on people, lulling them to sleep and their ultimate demise. Some of the symptoms of this gas are **lightheadedness, irritability, dryness of the nose or mouth, watering eyes** and a **sick feeling.** If you or anyone in the car begins to experience these symptoms take it very seriously. Often children sitting in the back of a car will begin to be affected by these symptoms first. If they are ignored, it can lead to tragedy.

Pull over and get out immediately. Breathe some fresh air, then roll the car windows down and proceed to a repair shop for an inspection. Obviously, something like this should be fixed right away. If you suspect this problem, keep the car windows open when driving to the shop.

> **Caution!** Never warm up your car in the garage with the door closed. The deadly gas quickly fills a small area and can kill an unsuspecting victim.

Now that you know the importance of a properly functioning exhaust system, have it inspected regularly for problems. It is easy to see how a garage could talk a car owner into spending unnecessary money. They know and you know that, like the brake system, the exhaust system must be in good order for safety reasons.

Fortunately, there are tons of big chain muffler specialty shops that are very competent and fast at doing exhaust repairs, plus a wide assortment of other garages that do this repair routinely. It takes very little time to get a free inspection and estimate from one of these shops, once the car is raised on a hoist. Usually the mechanic will call you over to look under the car so he can show you what the problem is. Because you can see the exhaust system and it is simple, you will be able to follow what the mechanic is saying.

Knowing the basics about the exhaust system is not difficult. Anyone can have a reasonable level of understanding. Do not be put off by the terms. You do not have to remember them, simply read this section before going to the muffler shop. Not looking perplexed by what the mechanic says will also prevent you from appearing to be an easy target and may discourage a fraud attempt.

The exhaust system is made up of several different connected parts. The **exhaust manifold** directs gases from the engine. Usually nothing goes wrong with the exhaust manifold and it is not normally referred to in everyday exhaust repairs. It is expensive to repair. From there the gases are sent into the **exhaust pipe** where the most poisonous are filtered through the **catalytic converter**. The sound of the engine is muffled by the **muffler** (finally a name that makes sense) and the remaining gases are expelled into the air via the **tailpipe,** which sticks out the back of the car.

Normal exhaust repairs deal with one or more of these parts: exhaust pipe, catalytic converter, muffler or tailpipe. On most cars these pieces can be replaced individually. Unscrupulous shops will try and sell a car owner more parts than they really need. On some cars the exhaust pipe, muffler and tailpipe are all one piece with the catalytic converter attached. Even in this case, shops can often remove one piece for replacement, instead of replacing the whole thing. It should be noted that the shops may try and sell you the whole shebang because they are all connected to each other. If there is damage to the entire system this is wise, but if the problem is isolated to a small section of the exhaust system, this can be an unnecessary expense. Simply ask them about cutting and welding in a new piece where the problem is. If a shop flatly refuses, or comes up with a multitude of reasons why they can't do this (other than the other parts are in need of replacement also) it is wise to check around. This is the beauty of the exhaust system – you can usually see the rust hole or crack that is causing the problem, giving you a clear picture of the truth if you know what to look for. It is surprising that car manufacturers haven't yet put a computer chip somewhere insied the exhaust pipe so the average driver would have no way of knowing what the problem is.

The **exhaust pipe** is attached to the bottom of the car with several brackets. The most common problem with the exhaust pipe, and the rest of the exhaust system for that matter, is that it rusts. If you live in a harsh climate, snow, rain and salt in the air or on the street will speed up the rusting process, slowly eating away at the exhaust system.

Many people do not know that a major contributor to rust is condensation occurring inside the exhaust system. This happens when the car is not warmed up properly for short trips in cold weather. Avoiding this type of driving can increase the life of the exhaust system.

Even the car's normal function creates an acidic water inside the exhaust system that eats away at the metal over time. It therefore makes sense that a "little" rust is not cause for a repair as there will almost always be some present. Holes, cracks or thin metal that can be poked through are unacceptable and cause for repair. There should never be any leaks in the system where harmful gases can escape. No gases should escape from the pipes other than out the end where they are supposed to, outside the car. It may be helpful to imagine that instead of gas, water is flowing through the pipes. There should not be any areas that the water would be able to drip out of the pipes.

The **catalytic converter** has the purpose of decreasing the amount of poisonous gas the car gives off into the atmosphere. It contains two special elements which coat the inside of the converter. When these elements come in contact with exhaust fumes, a reaction takes place which reduces the amount of poisonous emissions. The details of this reaction are not important, but that it works properly most certainly is. Lead and other additives in gasoline can poison the converter elements and render them ineffective, so it is important to always use unleaded gasoline (leaded gasoline, though no longer sold in Canada at regular gas stations, is still available in some other countries). A catalytic converter should last about 50 000 km, however it is usually difficult to tell if one is shot just by looking at it, unless there is obvious damage like a hole or extremely damaged metal. If a mechanic reports that you need a new catalytic converter because of surface rust, you may be getting ripped off. It is worth noting that some older cars do not even have catalytic converters, therefore if you don't own one of these, don't get charged for one anyway!

The **muffler** is also a simple device. It is designed to reduce noise and sparks. Without it the car would sound like a roaring street bike. Simply put, if your car is waking up the neighbors, get the muffler checked. Today, many cars have the muffler attached to the exhaust pipe; however it can be cut out and replaced individually without changing the rest of the exhaust system if it is the only part with a problem.

The main problem with the muffler is it rusts. Many people damage their muffler or even other parts of the exhaust system by speeding over bad road conditions. Speed bumps or small hills in the road can come in contact with and damage the exhaust system unless they are driven over slowly and carefully. If you see someone driving along with their muffler dangling by a thread or left on the road behind them, this may be what happened.

When driving on gravel or dirt roads at high speeds the tires can propel rocks underneath the car like bullets and damage the muffler. Less serious damage can occur when driving very fast on a bumpy road or even just from normal car vibration over time. This can throw the exhaust system out of whack by loosening things or shifting them around. This type of a repair may be as simple as tightening a clamp. Don't get talked into a major repair for something like this.

Similarly, if you often drive over really bumpy roads or fear the muffler has hit something, pull in once in a while and have a mechanic check that everything is tightly fastened. This can save money in the long run, preventing the muffler from falling off or becoming dragged and damaged.

It is wise to watch the mechanic very closely during this inspection. If a shop will not let you into the service area to observe the mechanic during the inspection, go somewhere else. Many shops don't want to let people into the service area for insurance reasons. However, an inspection is hardly a dangerous operation. Many shops will invite you to watch the inspection, but require you to leave during repairs for safety reasons (exhaust repairs often require welding). One case was reported where a mechanic was caught hammering holes into a perfectly good muffler so that he could sell the car owner a new one! Most mufflers will have some surface rust and a mechanic may poke at it to make sure it has not rusted through. A mechanic should not be hammering away at a muffler with great force to try and puncture the metal. Because of the surface rust already present, a crooked mechanic could actually trick a car owner who wasn't there for the inspection into thinking the rust was the real culprit.

Mufflers are sold with warranties, often lifetime ones. It is always a good idea to get the best warranty possible on any parts or labor. The problem is some shops look at warranties not only as an initial sales tool but also as a way to get you back for repeat business. Sure, they will replace the muffler for free, but they will also charge a fortune for additional parts and labor. Some times the shop will actually try and force you to have the other repairs done in order to claim the free muffler replacement. Always read the fine print on a warranty before you buy into it – then there will be no surprises. If you do go to claim a free muffler on a warranty and are presented with a high estimate for other associated repairs and labor, then it is a good idea to go to try some other shops and compare the price and work required without the warranty. It may turn out to be cheaper.

The **tailpipe** sticks out of the back of the car. It directs the fumes out and away from under the car. Tailpipes come in all styles and can be purchased at specialty stores if you want a little extra, like chrome plating.

The innocent tailpipe is sometimes used by the crooked mechanic to convince someone they need costly exhaust repairs. The mechanic plugs the tailpipe while the car is running and then draws attention to what appears to be a leak in the exhaust system. If the leak is from a hole, the part should be replaced. If it is simply a leak at one of the joints in the system, it may only require tightening a bolt.

It is also important to make sure that all the parts of exhaust system fit tightly together. When you try and move one piece of the system all the others should move with it as if it were one piece. If not, tightening clamps or making some other minor adjustment may be all that's required.

Caution! When inspecting the muffler system don't touch any parts until you are sure they have cooled off. The system operates at extremely high temperatures and you could easily burn yourself.

Exhaust Smoke

Smoke from the tailpipe comes in three colors. Take note of the colors that are acceptable – when in doubt obtain a second opinion from a professional.

Occasional **white smoke** when starting a car is normal. The problem is when there is a large cloud of white smoke spewing continuously out of the tailpipe. This indicates that the **gasket** in the engine that prevents the coolant from entering the cylinders has worn away and now coolant is leaking into the engine (see our section on the cooling system). Inside, the high engine heat evaporates the coolant and it is subsequently sent out as an unburned gas. Sometimes you can smell antifreeze from the exhaust. You should take the car to a mechanic immediately.

This type of repair is *very expensive*, due to the amount of labor involved. The mechanic needs to dismantle most of the upper engine components to get at the gasket and it's the labor you pay for. It is usually caused by driving a car with an overheated engine for too long or simply by an extremely overheated engine. You can avoid this damage by maintaining the car's cooling system and driving at reasonable speeds as conditions indicate.

This should not be confused with the normal white vapor that pours out of the tailpipe in very cold weather. If you are not sure about this, compare your car to others nearby. If your car is behaving differently than the rest, you obviously have a problem.

Blue smoke coming from the tailpipe is a sign that the car is burning oil. This is associated with a problem with either **piston rings** or **engine valves**, both of which you want to prevent from wearing out too soon. Regular maintenance is the best type of prevention. This includes regular oil changes to protect the inside of the engine.

Black smoke means there is too much fuel entering the **combustion chamber**. If you have a fuel-injected car it's just a matter of adjusting a few screws. With older carburetor engines, this requires a few minor adjustments and cleaning the **carburetor**. Fix these problems as soon as possible, if not for the car, then at least for the environment's sake.

Most parts in the exhaust system will need to be replaced every three to four years depending on how inviting the climate you live in is to rust. In this case, you will probably do well to go to a big chain specialty shop. They are fast and convenient, having all parts in stock so you can drive in and out quickly. If they don't stick you for unneeded work (which should be tougher as you have read this section), they should also be reasonably priced.

Brakes

Here's the scenario: you are driving down a side street. When stopping at the next red light, you hear a loud, screeching sound of metal rubbing against metal from outside. You wonder why the other driver doesn't get his worn brakes repaired. You look around and see no one but yourself. You continue to drive along and by the next traffic light realize that it's your car screeching at every stop. You feel embarrassed, but drive on.

Suddenly, right in front of you is a brake and muffler shop! There is a sign out front advertising a free brake inspection, and better still, a $99.99 special. This is a big name company, so you feel safe and pull in. You tell the mechanic about the screeching sounds and that you would like the free inspection and estimate. He tells you to come back in an hour, so you go to the donut shop (which is always next door) feeling relaxed because at worst it will cost $99.99.

When you return the mechanic hands you an estimate for over $450 in repairs. Your car is still hanging in the air with the wheels off, while the friendly mechanic explains all the problems that were found. Fortunately, they can begin work right away. When you point to the sign reading $99.99 and question the high estimate, the mechanic shows you the $99.99 mixed in with the other numbers on the estimate and states, "that is why it is so cheap. " What do you do? Often people in this situation feel relieved that the shop is able to fix the problem right away despite the high cost. From there they tend to authorize the repair and think they are getting off lucky.

This is a common scene and one you want to avoid. If you find yourself in this situation, there is something you can do to lessen the drain on your wallet. You have in your power the ability to say "yes" or "no" to the repair. With this in mind, tell the mechanic that the price is way too much and it will have to wait until another day. The mechanic will surely come back with a counter-proposal. Again say that it is too much and suggest that they do it for a more reasonable cost or you will leave. By this time they may give you a lower price and you can get a fair deal if you authorize the work. The best position to be in here is if you are familiar with the type of repair needed and the approximate cost that is reasonable. Without this information you are still risking paying more than you would somewhere else.

Getting the brakes repaired is a tricky business. You don't want to take any chances for safety reasons. The problem is the shops know this and will sometimes try and scare you into getting unneeded work at high prices. The importance to safety and the opportunity to make a dollar have made brake repairs one of the most common and expensive of all the different automotive repairs. The shops know full well that most drivers would not and *should not* take chances on faulty brakes. When in doubt, get them fixed.

Before getting into brake repairs there is one thing that you should do on a regular basis: when you are checking the oil, glance over at the **brake fluid reservoir (master cylinder)** and make sure it is full. (If you are not sure where it is, consult your manual.) Normally it looks like a square shallow box by the engine fire wall. When you open it you will notice the plastic or metal cap is inset with a rubber piece. When it pops out it means more fluid is needed.

It is best to not keep opening up the master cylinder to check the level of the brake fluid. The sides of the reservoir are often somewhat see-through and the level can be detected from just looking at it. When brake fluid is lost it should be replaced, but a steady loss of fluid indicates a problem is present and time for an inspection. When adding or checking fluid it is best to keep the lid closed as much as possible to prevent ruining the brake fluid.

When brake fluid is exposed to the air for long periods of time it loses some of its hydraulic properties and this can lead to weaknesses in the brake system. For this reason it is a good idea to have the brake system drained and flushed every time you suspect contamination. It is a good idea to do this when getting a major brake job. Another important thing to remember is to avoid getting any water inside the brake fluid reservoir.

Regardless of which garage you go to, there will usually be the famous **brake inspection**. There is normally no charge for the brake inspection and if someone attempts this, *go somewhere else*. You can expect to have the car raised up on a hoist and all the wheels removed to facilitate a thorough inspection. Many shops will be more than eager to inspect the brakes regardless of why you are in their shop. If your brakes are trouble free and have recently been serviced you may be better off paying them *not* to do a free inspection. It may be cheaper!

It is important to have some understanding of the brake system in order to follow what a mechanic is telling you during an inspection. Most cars have **disc brakes** in the front and **drum brakes** on the rear, although there are cars that have disc brakes or drum brakes on both front and rear. Simply put, both braking systems rely on linings to push up against something attached to the wheel and create friction to stop the car.

In the **disc braking system**, these linings are called **brake pads**. The pads are held in a clamp, called a **caliper**, that wraps around a **disc** (rotor). When you apply the brakes, the caliper squeezes the pads onto the rotor to stop the car. **Drum brakes** also stop the car by the use of linings, but these are called **shoes**. The brake drum itself looks like a big cooking pan. Inside the drum are two pieces of metal that each wrap half way around the inside of the pan – these are the brake shoes. These shoes have a cylinder in the middle which pushes them against the drum, and the contact brings the car to a stop.

As both pads and shoes are subject to friction and wear, they eventually need to be replaced. When you hear that loud squealing sound of metal on metal, mentioned earlier, every time the brakes are applied, it is usually due to front brake pads that have worn low. Some brake linings on newer cars are designed to squeal like this as a warning to change them. If a driver were to ignore this and continue driving, over time the disc would be damaged and a very expensive replacement required.

Sometimes minor screeching is due to dust and a sort of sheen forming over the brake pad. This can be easily sanded off and does not require new pads. If the screeching is persistent, have the pads checked.

Those are good reasons to always check to make sure the linings are really worn out before replacing them. An unscrupulous mechanic may be more than happy to let you believe they are shot in order to make an extra dollar, only cleaning them up and then charging you for a replacement. Always inspect the parts in question before and after a replacement to ensure the work has been done. If worn linings are the problem they should be relatively inexpensive and easy to replace. They are ready to be replaced when they are at about 35% of the original thickness (ask your dealer for the thickness specifications for your model).

When is a lining worn? Take a look at a new brake lining if you are unsure.

When the lining needs changing it will be about the same thickness as the metal backing it is attached to.

The only other reason for replacing brake linings is when brake fluid or grease has fouled them, which destroys their ability to create friction and reduces your braking power.

Drum shoes are usually a little thinner than pads when new, but they can also wear very thin before a problem arises. There are metal rivets in the shoes that will protrude when the linings wear thin. **These rivets should never be allowed to touch the drum.** If this metal is touching the drum you will likely hear a metallic grinding noise – take care of it immediately to prevent more serious damage. Both discs and drums are expensive. When in doubt it makes no sense to risk damaging them in order to save money on the less expensive pads and shoes.

Imagine driving to work and hearing a grinding sound every time you apply the brakes. If you were to take the car in to the shop the next day all you would have to pay for is a set of brake pads and the required labor. The result: a minimal charge of around $80. If you kept putting it off and driving to work daily for the next two weeks before you made time to get to the shop, the story would be different. This time the mechanic might inform you that you've damaged the rotors and they need replacing. A bill of $279. Why so much? Because rotors are expensive and there's more labor involved. Here you went from $80 to $279 in a couple of weeks. This is quite common among car owners. Many people pretend the noise in their car will go away, just like a headache might. Unfortunately, cars aren't self-repairing like humans, so look after your car when you notice symptoms, not when it breaks down.

The **calipers** also need service from time to time. If you are getting a full brake job this should definitely be included in the deal. You will save money having them rebuilt instead of having them replaced and normally this is more than adequate. Another item that can usually be rebuilt, at much less cost than replacement, are the **wheel cylinders** (inside the brake drums). It is more than worth while to ask if the cylinder can be rebuilt rather than replaced. This can be considerably cheaper than the new part, but not all shops offer this service.

On occasion, a brake cylinder can begin to leak badly and it is important to fix as soon as possible. It is not unusual to find a very small amount of brake fluid on the wheel cylinder. A small leak is not harmful and can be left alone. Mechanics will assuredly try to get your consent to rebuild the cylinders with even the tiniest leak, saying things like, "it can go at any minute" or "the brakes won't be as effective without it."

Mechanics may even go as far as to take a flathead screwdriver and pull back the rubber seal to show you the leak. This act in itself can damage the seal and let out fluid which will now justify his reason for changing them.

Use common sense – if there is visible fluid dripping out constantly then have them tended to, but if there is a little stain around the seal think twice, as it's normal.

Most of the braking power in a vehicle, about 70 percent, is derived from the front brakes and these are typically disc brakes. Even if the braking power in the rear brakes is reduced slightly it won't make much of a difference. If the threat of the rear brakes is more serious – such as possible "seizing" of the cylinder (seizing means grinding to a stop, preventing proper operation of the brakes) – then you will want to weigh all options and associated costs.

Three important tips to follow when going to the brake shop:

1. Don't panic. Tell the mechanic you didn't expect such a high price and have to talk with your spouse, or make some other polite excuse. Thank him for the free inspection and ask him for a detailed written estimate you can take with you. If he gives you a written estimate with each part and associated labor listed and its cost, this is a good sign. People who are lying and trying to cheat you will be hesitant to put the details of their scam down in writing or on company letterhead. Don't settle for just a few numbers written on a scrap of paper. Ask for a computer printout of their estimate. Getting a written estimate is an important step in checking out the shop's integrity. It is also important to have when shopping around, so that you can be sure exactly what work each shop feels is necessary and that you are comparing price for the same service.

Some shops will amaze you by suddenly offering a better price and trying to stop you from leaving with lengthy explanations and pressure sales tactics. *Make sure you leave with the best price in writing.* You *can* bargain with the majority of shops on price. You can then always return for the work at that price, if it turns out after further checking to be the best place.

---

2. Listen to what the mechanic says. Watch what he shows you, in regard to what needs fixing and why. Not only will this help you to learn about the car, it will give you a comparison for the next mechanic's advice. For example, if one shop wants to replace a part and the other shop feels it is fine, you can gather information

from both mechanics to make a better decision. Often a common sense solution will become obvious after hearing both arguments. Another possibility is to call a friend who has experience with car repairs and ask for an opinion. If you don't mind doing a little research, there are many books on basic automotive repair in the library.

3. Go to a more than one brake shop and get another free inspection, detailed estimate and explanation. You will be amazed at the different stories you may get, not only about what needs to be repaired, but also how it should be done and what the cost will be. You can sometimes save a hundred dollars on the identical work by shopping around. Another option, once you have determined what work needs to be done, is to call a few shops out of the telephone book and ask them what they would charge for the particular repair your car needs. You will often get lower prices by doing this, because the shop assumes you know what's going on and they don't already have your car up on the hoist.

Caution! If a mechanic says that you have a dangerous problem with the brakes or any other car part that prevents you from driving around and getting a second opinion, you have only one defense – knowledge about your car. Common sense dictates that if the brakes are seriously failing the car should be stopped immediately to avoid an accident. If the brakes are only squealing a bit, shop around.

Always try and fix the brakes right away, as the problem can only get worse, more expensive and more dangerous. The key is not to wait until a problem becomes so bad that the car is a danger on the road or impossible to drive around for different estimates. If you need to be towed to a shop the cost of repair will be very high. They know they have you! The shop is aware that the cost of towing the car to another shop and the uncertainty of what they will say gives them a distinct advantage.

It is worth the time when getting a brake job to watch the mechanic work, to make sure that the cylinders and calipers are tended to properly. Even if you don't know what he is doing, he doesn't know that and it shouldn't be hard to tell if he is actually servicing something or just wiping it off. In addition, you have first-hand proof of everything they do.

Remember this: if you need new brake pads and no logical reason is presented to do any other work, then it makes sense to get new pads only.

It is always advisable to replace pads and shoes in pairs.

When you are convinced that some other work will be needed in the near future, it is probably better to get it all done at once in order to save money, hassle and improve safety.

If you go in for a brake repair it is not uncommon to be told that your rotors or drums need to be *machined*. Machining is simply another way of saying smoothing out the rough metal. Often this is done when it is not needed. To machine or not to machine, that is the question. If there are circular grooves worn into the rotors deep enough to snag a fingernail on, or if dark spots are present, machining is required.

Keep in mind that too much machining can actually wear out your rotors or drums.

In reality, consenting to unnecessary machining is really paying the shop to help wear out the drums and rotors so that you will have to eventually buy expensive new ones.

In order to protect yourself, always do the nail scratch test beforehand. Tell the mechanic to measure the thickness of the drums or rotors both before and after machining and have him record it on the receipt for you. There are specific safety standards set by law that need to be adhered to (see your dealer or brake shop for details). Once a rotor or drum is too thin they run the risk of cracking under braking pressure.

Another safety consideration when machining drums or discs is the issue of visible cracks or dark blue spots. Small cracks sometimes appear on a disc or drum and are called **crazing**. Brakes operate under high pressure and friction, producing a substantial amount of heat. Crazing cracks are caused by the constant expansion and contraction of the metal. When the cracks are mild, machining can temporarily solve the problem, but upon more continuous braking, the cracks may become much worse and possibly very dangerous.

Similarly, blue spots or patches on the discs or drums are also caused by too much heat. The blue metal is actually hardened by excessive heat and is no longer appropriate for safe braking. Once again, in mild forms, the blue patches can be machined away. Opinions are mixed on this practice. Some mechanics feel that when either "spotting" or "crazing" occurs the safest option is to replace the affected parts. One thing is certain, when either severe crazing or spotting occur, replacement is the only safe option!

But to avoid the expense of replacing parts, don't get talked into unnecessary machining. Often a shop will try and sell a customer on a brake special that includes machining. Without thinking, the customer will agree and the mechanic will machine the drums and/or discs, whether they need it or not – especially if you are watching, in order to justify the charge. This is doing more harm than good. Again, machining is only required when a disc or drum surface is grooved or lightly spotted. Most often cracks or heavy spotting are cause for replacement. Do not be talked into machining for other reasons without a second opinion. A disc that has been overserviced and machined too thin can eventually break and cause an accident.

On the other side of the coin, package deals include a machining charge. Since most cars don't need it, the shop can avoid the service and save money. In this situation it may be wiser to just pay for the work that the car needs and not the brake package.

When you do feel those grooves or see those dark spots it should be noted that proper machining involves two steps. The first step does the bulk of the job and is always done. However, the second step, or finishing step, makes the job much better but requires more time on the part of the mechanic and is often left out. To make sure that this step is performed, it would not hurt to ask the mechanic, "Please be sure to include a fine cut on the lathe."

An important and often overlooked area in a brake job is to carefully inspect the brake hoses. Any cracks or other signs of weakness or deterioration are good reason to replace them. The fluid moves through these hoses at an extremely high pressure and any weaknesses can quickly worsen. These hoses are sometimes cut by an unscrupulous mechanic who later shows you that they need to be replaced. This is another good reason to watch the mechanic as he does the brake job if at all possible, or at the least to be around for the initial inspection.

The final key to repairing the brakes properly and avoiding extra expense is: do not wait until they are so bad that it is dangerous to drive them around for different opinions. Have them regularly inspected, definitely at the first sign of trouble. Signs are the sounds of metal grinding and squealing. Noticing that the brake pedal is almost touching the floor, brake power is weaker than normal and consistently low brake fluid in the reservoir should motivate you to get cracking and find out what the problem is with the car. Keeping on top of brake repairs will not only save you money, but possibly avoid an accident.

Shocks and Suspension

Your suspension provides you with a comfortable ride. It controls the up and down movement caused by driving on uneven road surfaces. It is also a key factor in road handling and is what keeps your car on the road when turning corners. Steering and braking are greatly affected by the type of suspension system you have. A good suspension system will improve braking because of increased road traction. This could make the difference between stopping in an emergency situation or sliding right into a car that has stopped in front of you. One sign of wearing shocks is excessive or more noticeable bounce when going over bumps. When you feel yourself being pushed forward against the steering wheel and the front of the car dips down in short-distance braking situations, this is a common sign of a worn suspension.

Most late model cars have **independent suspension**. This means that each wheel will respond to a dip or bump in the road independent of what the other wheels are doing and without affecting the other three tires. To protect the car, a number of springs were incorporated, used to absorb the rising and falling motion that a car experiences when it hits a pothole or speed bump. Springs were not meant to be changed regularly, and are usually trouble free. However, if it were left up to the springs your car would keep bouncing up and down for a long time after you hit the bump. This is where the shocks come in. These devices control the bounce and return your car to a level motion. The faster and smoother they can achieve this, the better and newer they are. As they wear their absorbing ability fades. Again, avoid potholes and street curbs whenever possible.

Shock absorbers usually cannot be disassembled, refilled or adjusted. They normally have to be replaced when they wear out. There are four basic types of shocks; **regular, heavy duty, gas-powered** and **Macpherson struts**. Many other names have been given to these four types, but those are manufacturers' product names. Buy shocks according to need. Not every car requires heavy duty gas-powered shocks, so ensure you receive the proper shocks for your driving life.

Ask yourself some basic questions when you are considering replacing the shocks. Are you hauling heavy loads? Are you often driving large groups of people around? If you are, you need to consider buying heavy duty or gas-powered shocks to be able to handle the extra loads. Are you looking for optimal car performance? Do you admire Mario Andretti? In this case you will want to look into gas-powered shocks and replacing the springs on your car with stiffer ones. These will give you better road handling at the cost of a bumpier ride.

If you have a front wheel drive, then your vehicle will need Macpherson struts. These are more expensive to replace and are complete units of shocks and springs that are used only on front wheel drive cars.

Sometimes you can just replace the shock inside, so check with a mechanic before spending alot of money on Macpherson struts.

In order to make sure that the shocks and springs are in good shape, there are a few things you should check:

1. Take a close look at the wear on the tires. If you notice uneven or adverse tire wear, a problem may exist. Check the tire itself, tire pressure, wheel balancing and suspension before getting a wheel alignment done or replacing the shocks.

2. Perform a bumper test to estimate wear on shocks. Push down hard on the corner of the bumper a few times and let go; if your car bounces more than two to three times before leveling out, this indicates fading of the shocks. Perform this exercise on the four corners to obtain a total analysis of your vehicle.

3. When you are driving and you turn a corner, do you feel like you are being thrown to the other side of the

vehicle? Did it cause your friend to spill his coffee everywhere? These are common signs of shock wear. Keep in mind that your car may be equipped with inferior shocks. There is no need to rush to the suspension mechanic, but you should stop driving the family car like a sports machine.

4. When you are required to make a safe stop, does you car take a considerable distance to stop, or skid easily? If this is the case check the brake system. If you have to make an immediate stop your car will end up skidding into the accident. With fairly new brakes this shouldn't happen and if it does, you should check the shocks.

Older cars have **suspension joints** that need periodic grease refilling. You may have heard of the old lube job at the local oil and lube shop. If your car needs this service, ask your mechanic, then make sure that the joints are always filled with grease. Otherwise, these important joints will wear prematurely.

On newer cars, the joints have been sealed so you don't need a "lube job." Avoid being charged for this when you have the oil changed. This happens often since most people aren't aware of what mechanics do underneath their car.

Also, some people get talked into changing their shocks on a relatively new vehicle to cure a vibration of some sort. It is an unnecessary expense because other parts of a car can often rub together. It may just be the inner molding in your car is shifting, causing an annoying sound. Replacing the shocks won't help.

Wheel Alignment and Tire Maintenance

Through the course of driving your vehicle in all kinds of weather and road conditions, your vehicle's steering components may become misaligned. Driving into potholes and over curbs are two of the fastest ways to offset the wheel alignment. As a vehicle gets older and steering components wear, the alignment will deteriorate, affecting the tire wear and steering control and determining how safe your vehicle is to drive. Imagine your car pulling to the left as you forcibly try to turn right or the front of the vehicle shaking violently while braking on wet and icy roads. These situations can contribute to an accident.

When you notice your car pulling to one side on a level road it's time to stop and have it looked at. Other signs include the steering wheel shaking while driving at higher speeds or the vehicle vibrating as you apply the brakes: indications that your car needs a visit to the mechanic. These problems will affect the wear on the tires and very often leave the tires unevenly worn and in need of replacement.

Without a doubt, before going to any shop for one of these problems, check the tire pressure. Having an over- or under-inflated tire can make your car act very strangely, often pulling to one side or the other.

If your car is a front wheel drive you will need a **four-wheel alignment**. Some late model cars and luxury sedans also require a four-wheel alignment because of their independent suspension system. This will require the use of special equipment and a trained technician. These are more expensive than a two wheel alignment. Most cars with rear wheel drive will require a two-wheel alignment. You can usually find coupons or specials for wheel alignments inside the local papers.

Check with your car's manual if you are not sure and have this information before going to a mechanic. This will protect you from being charged for a four-wheel alignment when only two are needed.

Specialty tire and alignment shops adjust wheel alignments daily and should do a good job. They must be able to do good quality alignments, because when they sell tires and do an alignment, they want the tires to last because of the warranty. Often shops will try and sell you a wheel alignment when all you need is **wheel balancing**. If an alignment is needed it is a good idea to get it done as soon as possible in order to prevent tire damage and the need for new tires. When an alignment shop tries to sell you extra parts on top of the alignment, be careful, especially if the alignment is offered at a cheap price. A really unscrupulous shop may try to talk you into buying a new (and unnecessary) set of tires to fix a minor problem. B&S may be happening. An alignment machine is expensive and to make a profit on doing alignments, they may try and sucker you in for additional unnecessary parts and labor.

When the tires are out of balance the steering wheel vibrates while driving at high speeds. **Balancing tires** is a simple act of placing tiny weights on the rim to centre the balance. If it is not centred, the wheel wobbles and will wear all steering and suspension parts. Premature suspension wear, excessive tire wear or possible tire tread damage, and a damaged wheel bearing could result.

If you are afraid of getting a flat tire on the highway because you don't know what to do then its important to learn how to change one. Ask a friend to show you how to change it or get out the owner's manual and practice changing the tire. This is much safer and less stressful than trying to figure it out on the road on a rainy night.

Most vehicles today are equipped with a **space-saver tire** in the trunk. This is a temporary replacement tire that is smaller and deflated to save space. A small air canister is used to inflate it when it's needed. You will have to replace the canister after each use. The life-span of this tire is about 3 000 miles. Just use it to get you home safely then have the proper tire repaired. The space-saver is not designed to handle extreme driving conditions or high speeds, so take the slow lane home.

If a tire keeps losing air, it can be from many causes. Don't just replace it. Try to have the mechanic find the cause if it's not obvious. For example, a nail stuck in the tire can be fixed for a nominal cost. The mechanic can always patch the tire if the damage is not too severe. This is much cheaper than buying a new tire. Sometimes the **tire valve** (used to inflate or deflate the tire) has a leak. Put some soap and water into the hole of the valve and watch for any bubbles that may appear. If there are bubbles, then the valve can either be tightened or replaced. You can get a mechanic to fix this for you for only a few dollars.

If the valve is not the problem, then have the tire tested for leaks at a garage. Watch the mechanic as he tests the tire. This will keep him honest as he doesn't know what you do or do not know. Don't ask questions, just watch quietly. Many tests are simple, like submerging the tire to find the leak.

For maintenance, have the tires rotated. Tires can be rotated in 24 000 km intervals to achieve their maximum life-span, although this option isn't vitally necessary.

Air Conditioner

Normally the air conditioner is considered a luxury – unless you live in Arizona during the summertime. Therefore, you can take your time getting the best information and price for a repair (unlike bad brakes). Don't take the air conditioner to be repaired or serviced on the hottest day of the year. For some reason, this situation makes shops feel they can charge more because of the demand.

As with any type of car repair, looking desperate is bad for your wallet. It's like getting a glass of water; normally it's free and you can get some almost anywhere. But if you're in the middle of the desert, dying of thirst, that same glass of water can be worth a lot to you and the waterseller knows you will pay almost anything for it.

Think about this with all of your automotive repairs. Always refrain from looking and acting desperate, no matter how you may be feeling, as this is a sure way to make the price go through the roof. The more calm, carefree and businesslike you are, the more likely you are to be treated as such. Saying things like "Thank goodness you were open!", "Whatever it takes, I just need it done right away!" or "I can't stand to drive without my air conditioning another moment!" gets the little cash register in their heads dinging away.

It may sound obvious, but if the air conditioner is working at an acceptable level, resist being pulled in for one of those summertime specials to try and get the air conditioner working a tiny bit better. If you have this much time and money on your hands, volunteering for a charity would be much more productive and gratifying. These service specials usually entail more **refrigerant** being added to the air conditioning system. The problem is, in many cases, too much refrigerant in the system can actually *reduce* the cooling effect more than having too little would.

This is why cooling systems are sometimes weaker after servicing, even if their air conditioner was originally working at an acceptable level. Since no one is going to be killed by a sudden air conditioner failure, it makes sense to leave well enough alone and saving repairs for when they are really needed.

To help prevent future problems with the air conditioner, it is a good idea to run it for a few minutes every once in a while, even in the winter. When it isn't used for long periods of time, even during the cooler seasons, the inside of the system can dry out and deteriorate, causing all sorts of leaks and problems.

The added bonus to firing up the air conditioner once in a while is if ever there is a problem with it, you have plenty of time to get it repaired at your leisure. Also remember the seasonal surcharge.

When the air conditioner is genuinely in need of repair, it is most often due to leaks in the system. Fixing the leaks usually requires replacing a leaky hose or seal and recharging the system with new **freon gas**. Another common and inexpensive problem is simply a blown **fuse** that needs to be replaced. The problem could simply be with the **compressor belt**. The compressor belt is near the **fan belt** and if you are not sure which one it is, check them all. The belts are those black rubber cords under the hood of the car joining different parts together. These belts should be checked regularly anyhow. If they appear cracked or worn, get them replaced as soon as possible as they are inexpensive, but a broken belt can leave you stranded somewhere at great inconvenience, possibly even at the expense of a tow, if you don't happen to have a spare in the trunk and the knowledge to change it.

The most expensive and least likely problem is needing a new **air conditioning compressor**. If a shop immediately tries to sell you a new compressor or convince you with some other reason why the air conditioner repair should cost a fortune, get a second opinion. It is quite difficult for the average person to be able to tell whether the mechanic is telling the truth when it comes to the air conditioning system, unless they have a better than average knowledge of their car. It is getting more and more difficult to figure out the electronically-complex modern vehicles that literally contain thousands of wires, hundreds of fuses, computer chips and a multitude of other gadgets. Anyone with an untrained eye will have great difficulty in determining where the problem lies.

Because of the many different parts to the air-conditioning system, it is quite easy for an unscrupulous mechanic to convince a customer that expensive repairs are needed when in fact they are not. For example, a common problem among air conditioners is a faulty **thermostat**. This results in the air conditioner working temporarily and then blowing hot air. A good place to begin searching for the problem is with the thermostat, and it is usually not difficult or expensive to fix. However, the mechanic may wish to try and sell you other repairs. Always remember: it's only the air conditioner. Get the standard estimate and second opinion.

Another common and inexpensive problem that can occur, especially after extended highway driving, is that the **condenser** becomes plugged. The condenser is located just in front of the radiator. Sometimes leaves and insects plug the condenser and cause the air-conditioning system to function poorly.

It is simple to clean out the condenser and well worth the while to ask a mechanic about checking and cleaning it. This might solve the problem without having to authorize any expensive servicing.

Some models of cars are equipped with a **sight glass** that enables you to tell if there is a problem with the air conditioner. A sight glass looks like a porthole. Check the car manual for its location. Only a limited selection of cars have them installed. They are quite simple to read and reflect the state of the freon gas in the air-conditioning system. Check the sight glass after the system has been running about five minutes and if it is still clear, the system is fine. A few bubbles inside may indicate that the system needs to be recharged. Many bubbles or foam could signify another problem, possibly a leak. If the glass is smudgy, then the system is likely not working at all.

This check does not completely isolate the problem, but will give you an idea of its severity and can be used as a starting point in determining the state of the air conditioner. Of course, since the sight glass is meant to help the driver know what is going on, certain crooked mechanics have found a way to use this information to scam unwary customers. The scam works like this.

The mechanic calls over the car owner and points out a few dreaded bubbles in the sight glass as evidence supporting the need for his services. The mechanic fails to tell the customer that even a well-charged air-conditioning system can have a few bubbles in the sight glass when the car is running cold. Once the car is warmed up and moved up in gear those same bubbles often disappear. When in the shop for an unrelated repair, a mechanic may try and convince you that the air conditioner you previously felt was working fine, needs service. It is worth your time to listen, but it is better to leave it alone when it is functioning properly.

Caution! The gases in the air-conditioning system are under high pressure and can be very dangerous if they come into contact with human skin. Serious and possibly irreversible damage can result. Therefore, if you know a little about cars and wish to visually inspect the system to find the problem, this is fine. Looking for leaks, loose wires or other obvious problems can save money, but don't try and do any repairs or tug on any hoses – it is just not worth it.

Many people don't realize that when an air-conditioning system is opened up for servicing it needs to be "evacuated" before refilling it with freon gas. In order to do this, certain equipment is needed specific to the job. Not all shops routinely offer this service.

Refilling the system without prior evacuation can lead to not only poorer air-conditioning performance, but also future problems that may not have otherwise occurred. It is wise to inquire whether or not the mechanic will do a proper evacuation when servicing the air conditioner.

As previously mentioned, the air-conditioner compressor is quite expensive and therefore should be well cared for. Whenever the air-conditioning system is serviced, the oil in the air-conditioning compressor should be checked and filled up if necessary.

Another practice that can damage a compressor is when a mechanic, due to a lack of the proper equipment, decides to evacuate the air-conditioning system by using the compressor. This can cause problems with the compressor and lead to high and unnecessary expenses down the road. It is worthwhile to politely inquire whether or not the mechanic intends to do this.

An example of how "improving" an air conditioner that is working well can balloon into a nightmare is not hard to find. One day Jake was driving by when he saw a sign for an inexpensive air-conditioner service package. It said, "Beat the Heat, with our Super Cool Service at Ice Age Prices." He was sold. He pulled in for this amazing special to improve his air conditioner, which he figured was probably operating at 80 percent of potential. The mechanic was friendly and started work immediately without asking Jake what the problem was. The mechanic came back to Jake and reported a few miscellaneous areas of wear that should be tended to, some worn hoses, in the spirit of avoiding future problems and getting better results. This boosted the bill, but Jake went for it.

Who knows, it could be true. Then the mechanic came back and said, "You know Jake, if I was you I would just put in a new compressor now, sure it's expensive, but I have a great deal on one for you. Yours will likely go anytime, besides, there is no point doing all this other work without going all the way, right?" Now the bill has rocketed into the hundreds, so Jake wisely said, "Forget it, I'll take my chances." So the disappointed mechanic finished the job, carelessly overfilling the system with refrigerant and failing to top up the oil in the compressor which was accidentally lost during servicing. Jake paid the bill (which with the extras was three times the advertised special) and hit the road. Now, due to too much refrigerant, the air conditioner was not working as well as it was before he went into the shop. Jake went back and the mechanic said, "I told you, you need a new compressor." (Which lost oil during the service operation and will likely wear out much sooner than it should have.) Moral of the story: unlike brakes, leaving the air conditioner well enough alone is a good idea until service is really needed.

Many people don't realize that the air-conditioning system affects the rest of the car. The air conditioner takes away power from the engine. This has several side effects: 1) poorer overall gas mileage when running the air conditioner and 2) an overheated engine on a sweltering day. The problem can be greatly intensified when the car is towing a trailer, another car or even just carrying a heavier than normal load. Turn off the air conditioner when putting extra strain on your car by going up a steep hill, especially when combined with the other conditions previously mentioned.

It is also advisable to leave the air conditioner off when cold starting the car. In contrast, on the highway it may be easier on the car and more fuel efficient to run the air conditioner rather than to open the windows. When driving at high speeds with the windows open, extra strain is put on the engine from the increased wind resistance on the back window and reduced streamlining of the car.

Heater

Depending on the part of the world you live in, the heater may or may not be of great concern. In some Northern cities, the heater is absolutely essential.

The car's interior heater works by diverting heat from the car's engine to warm the inside of the car. When the car is warmed up to a normal operating temperature there is no shortage of heat. Some of the heat from the hot engine coolant is redirected into a mini-radiator underneath the dashboard called the **heater core**. A fan blows air through the heater core into the passenger compartment to warm you up.

On older cars this system is quite simple and problems can be diagnosed fairly easily. However, as cars become more and more high-tech with computerized climate control and so on, finding the inexpensive problem can cost a fortune in labor. Rather than go to a shop where the mechanic is obviously perplexed, try a few different shops to see if someone can find the problem right away, before they start to charge for diagnostics. A common puzzler is the heater not working. Often the **thermostat** is malfunctioning, and this prevents any heater use at all because it will not turn on. This is normally easy to repair and inexpensive. The thermostat is usually a good place to start looking for the problem when the heater is acting up.

Similar to the air conditioner, the heater can have some negative effects on the rest of the car, even when functioning perfectly. As stated earlier, the interior heater draws heat away from the engine.

Leave the heater off until your car engine is completely warmed up. The initial warm-up period is one of the toughest on the engine. Using the heater at this point increases the wear on the engine.

Over time, seemingly small details like this one can add up to a much larger problem that could have been avoided. With a cold engine, the heater only blows cold air and this does little to warm the inside of the car.

It is also wise to run the heater for a short time every once in a while in the warmer seasons, as it keeps the heating system wet and ready to operate. Inactivity here, as in other parts of the car, over long periods of time can lead to problems.

It pays off to use the car's options once in a while, even if you really don't need to. This helps provide proper lubrication, prevents jamming and freshens the particular system. It also lets you know things are working. It is better to be aware when something doesn't work so that it can be fixed at your convenience, rather than being let down when you really need it.

Maintenance and Your Car

Maintaining your vehicle is the best way to ensure that it causes you the least amount of problems and breakdowns in the future. Most people wait until something breaks or loud screeching noises appear before they take it in for servicing, then they get upset when their repair bill is $200 more than they expected. Instead of waiting for something to happen, why not take an active role by doing some preventive maintenance and putting some money aside for the *inevitable* repairs your vehicle will need.

Remember what we mentioned in the beginning: your vehicle will give you apparent signs of a need for servicing. It will usually begin with dashboard lights flashing and then move on to squeals, clunks, screeching and so on. After this, you will either see smoke and liquid leaks or smell strange chemicals. If you wait past this point, serious damage could result to important mechanical components and this may make it dangerous to drive and expensive to fix.

Before you do anything else, set up an entry log for all the service done to your vehicle. When you fill it in, include what was repaired or changed and the date and location of the shop. You can even go so far as to comment about whether or not they did an acceptable and competitively priced repair. This log will help to eliminate many problems in finding what's troubling your car in the future. The mechanic can eliminate parts that are new and pinpoint the area that requires attention much quicker.

This alone can save you hours of paid labor. The repair log is even more useful if you are unfamiliar with the basic systems of your car, since your mechanic can decipher the language for you. Write down the technical language regarding the repair and show this to the mechanic. It is of no use to your mechanic to know that "you had the brakes done." They need to know specifically what was repaired and replaced, so don't leave things out.

The following is a list of the vital areas that need regular maintenance. They aren't the only parts that require service, but they are often overlooked and directly related to the extended life of your vehicle. Many of the services can be performed by the owner or with assistance from friends that have some general automotive mechanics knowledge.

List Of Common Neglected Vehicle Maintenance Areas:

1. Oil
   - ☐ The chemicals inside the oil break down over time and provide less protection. Also dirt and other deposits build up and could damage the internal components.
   - ☐ Most experts recommend changes every 4 800-9 600 km (more frequent changes under harsh driving conditions).
   - ☐ Alternatively, change oil every 3 to 6 months depending again on driving and environment.
   - ☐ Check oil periodically just to make sure it is there and at the right level.

2. Antifreeze
   - ☐ Check the level of coolant (antifreeze and water) at least once a month.
   - ☐ Coolant loses its protective ability after a couple of years, so change coolant every two years.
   - ☐ Do a "flush and fill" every other coolant change or more frequently under adverse conditions.
   - ☐ Replace thermostat every 2-3 years.

3. Tires
   - ☐ Maintain proper tire pressure.
   - ☐ Purchase a good tire gauge (cheap ones are very inaccurate) and use it instead of the service station's.
   - ☐ Check for uneven tire wear.

- [ ] Test tire pressure with cold tires that have been driven less than a mile or that have sat for a couple of hours (the local climate will be a factor in this estimate).

4. Brakes

- [ ] Have the brakes inspected (free of charge) every year. This can prevent any unforeseen problems and give you braking confidence while driving.
- [ ] Remember not to have any unneeded work done.

5. Steering and Suspension

- [ ] Inspect shocks for leaks.
- [ ] Have the suspension system greased when needed if you have an older vehicle.
- [ ] Check proper wheel alignment, this will save the tires.

6. Fluid Check

- [ ] Transmission fluid (change every 40 000 miles or km).
- [ ] Brake fluid (fill to maximum level).
- [ ] Coolant level (check radiator and reservoir level).
- [ ] Oil (change every 3 to 6 000 miles or 5 to 10 000 km).
- [ ] Power steering fluid (fill to level).
- [ ] Battery (electrolytic fluid level).
- [ ] Windshield washer fluid (fill to maximum).

7. Engine Inspection

- [ ] Alternator and fan belt – cracks and wear.
- [ ] Hoses – bulges, splits and cracks.
- [ ] Engine – leaks, oil patches.
- [ ] Radiator – leaks, green fluid.
- [ ] Air filter – dirt.
- [ ] Electrical connections – with engine off and key out of ignition check to make sure all electrical connections are properly connected.
- [ ] Excessive dirt and grease – cleaning this off will help the engine to run cooler.
- [ ] Windshield wipers – look for cracked or worn blades.
- [ ] Underneath car – check for oil spills, coolant leaks and transmission leaks.

8. Lights
- [ ] Have another person confirm that all the lights are in working order.
- [ ] While sitting in the car have them put the turning signals on, apply brake pedal, turn on the headlights and shift car into reverse with brakes applied.
- [ ] You should walk around the car and check if all the lights are in working order.

Section Three

The Extras

Tires

One of the most important pieces of equipment on your vehicle are the tires. A vehicle performs only as good as the tires on it. Many people will spend $500-$600 on the best stereo system, but insist on buying the cheapest set of tires they can find. This is not a wise choice if safety is important to you.

When shopping for a tire you will notice four basic varieties; **summer, winter, all season** and **high performance**. Summer tires are specifically designed for dry weather and normal road conditions. If they are used in extreme wet weather the treads may get filled with water and cause *hydroplaning*, where your tires are lifted clear of the road to skid on the surface of the water.

When there are long periods of wet and snowy weather, you will want to buy a set of winter tires. However, winter tires should not be driven in the summer as they do not allow you to drive at a comfortable driving speed and wear much faster than summer tires in dry weather.

Ideally, you would want to have a set of summer tires and rims and an extra set of winter tires and rims. It is a good idea to have two sets of rims because changing the tires every season can damage the seal or bead on the tire and could shorten their life-span.

All season tires provide good coverage for dry and wet road conditions, although they will not be as effective as using the specific seasonal tires. They are slightly more expensive than either the summer or winter tires, but give you comparable value if you take into account that you don't have to buy two sets of wheels. In addition, they avoid the hassle of changing and storing tires between seasons. Again, keep in mind the area you live in; in places in like Minnesota or Northern British Columbia, all season tires may be ineffective during their long, cold and snowy winters.

Car enthusiasts who enjoy and prefer optimum performance in dry weather will want to buy high performance tires. These, of course, are more expensive. The advantage to buying this type of tire over the others is better quality. The **side walls** are thicker to protect them from being damaged on the road. These tires also withstand higher driving temperatures and speeds on most types of dry and wet road conditions. Sometimes the extra cost is worth the safety it provides for your family, even if you don't drive like Andretti.

Think about getting the best tires you can afford – your car relies on the tires to stop, turn, carry heavier loads, cushion your ride and prevent you from sliding on ice. Even if you had the best brake system available, without good tires it would only function adequately. A mechanical part is only as good as its weakest support.

Bias ply, belted bias, radial tires, and **retreads** are the types of tires available today. Bias ply are becoming obsolete and belted bias are rapidly disappearing. Retreads are quite common, but not so much for cars as for semi-trailers and other machinery such as bulldozers and the like. The one attractive aspect is their price, which is normally 30-50 percent cheaper than new tires.

Most new cars today are factory-installed with radials. These are the preferred choice among the kinds available.

Caution! You should never combine the different types of tires together. Why? The internal belts are formed differently on a bias ply than a radial tire, so that when you drive with both types on the same car, the belts could tear and pose a great threat of a tire explosion while driving.

It is a common mistake to mix tire types, especially if you purchase used tires from private owners or from obscure shops who carry outdated inventory.

Where you can go to purchase a new set of tires for your car? Avoid new car dealers, since they sell tires at an unreasonably inflated price. Gas stations and service stations also are expensive and should be avoided. Try shopping for your tires at tire wholesalers or independent dealers, but deal with someone who knows what they are talking about. If they can't answer all your questions to your satisfaction, go somewhere else.

Two common selling techniques in any business are: pushing the item that makes the most money or getting rid of unwanted stock. The tires that the salesperson is pushing the most may not be the best ones for you. Shop around, talk to dealers and decide what is best for your vehicle before making any deals.

When you are ready to deal, try to get the mounting and balancing included, otherwise they will charge you an additional service fee. These fees can be as low as $10 per tire to as high as $25 per tire. That puts another $100 in your pocket.

It goes without saying that you don't want to buy a new set of tires when the old ones are fine. The main reason for replacing a set of tires is due to excessive **tread wear**. As the treads wear down, the tires become less effective. Mechanics have a special ruler to measure treads, but if at all possible have someone do it who does not sell tires. A trick to do this yourself is to use an old Lincoln headed penny or one with the Queen's head. Stick the penny into the tread with the head pointing down; if you can see his or her forehead the treads are too low. Keep in mind that this method only provides a rough estimate.

When buying new tires, the old ones from your vehicle may be traded in for a small sum, if they have some life left in them. The key word is small, because you won't get much money for them at the shop. A better option is to sell them off privately and get substantially more for them.

Some people even keep one or two as spares. The old tires are the right size for your vehicle and it would cost alot more to replace even a used tire to serve as a spare.

Another question about the cost of the tires is, how long they will last? If you consider that the new tires will last roughly 3 years or about 60 000 km then it doesn't seem all that unreasonable to spend $400 or $500 on a new set for your vehicle. The **tread wear rating** can give you a rough idea on the life of the tire. A grading of 300 is fairly high and logically will last twice as long as one with a rating of 150 under similar driving conditions. It also depends on what kind of driver you are and what kind of road conditions are present. The lower grade tire will be cheaper to buy, but the higher grade will generally perform better and provide more safety. When you think about a tire don't just think about safety, but also consider the lives of your family and that of other drivers and pedestrians. The last thing you want is to have an accident because of poor quality tires.

Other factors to look at are the **special load capacities** (how much weight the tires can carry) and the unique benefits of an **innovative tread design,** which can provide better traction in snow or channel out water on the road, or **sidewall.** A stiffer sidewall may protect your tire from being punctured by a foreign object on the road, and a thicker sidewall can make the tire less susceptible to flexing while turning corners and will provide better handling. Ask around to find out which companies have a solid reputation in the industry, not the ones that advertise the most. Also, avoid buying tires on sale or those which just look good: a tire may look like a performance tire until you check the specifications and feel the material. Don't just look at the image, display and trim, but check the specs thoroughly.

A mechanic can tell you alot about your tire by looking at the pattern of the tread wear, so whenever your car is on a hoist for anything, ask them to have a look at the tires. It doesn't cost you or them anything. This will give you information about the tires' state of repair so that you won't get ripped off by a crooked shop. Tires wear slowly over time.

For example, when getting her fan belt changed two months ago, Diane's mechanic told her the tires were fine with lots of life left in them. Now, when going into a tire shop to fix a flat, she is being told that all her tires are shot and need replacement. If she didn't have the free information from her mechanic, the tire shop could have tricked her into purchasing new tires over a year before she needed them.

When a tire is really shot and you are in the market for the new ones, it pays to understand "tire language." This will help you to compare different tires and their value. Look up the **traction value** that is assigned to the tire. A traction letter grade of A has the best traction; this tire will maintain excellent performance even in wet and slippery road conditions. The stopping distance is greatly affected by the traction rating of the tire. B is not as good as A and a C grade gives the worst traction of them all. Don't get caught with a tire rating of C on a wet road unless you want to teach your car to moonwalk.

Another important rating is the **temperature**. It relates to how the tire reacts to driving temperatures. When you drive, the friction caused by the rubber on the road increases the internal temperature of the tire. If a tire gets too hot it may fatigue and burst or the internal belts become damaged. A tire with an A rating will remain the coolest and is recommended for long distance and high speed driving. B is generally accepted and C is understandably avoided unless you are a slow and short distance driver.

One last consideration for the tire is the **speed rating**. These letters are useful in determining which type of tire will provide the best performance for your kind of driving. Also, for high speed drivers, they will permit you to choose the best tires for you to drive safely at the desired high speeds.

The following is a list of the top speeds for each grade:

S 112 mph (180 kph)

H 130 mph (210 kph)

V 149 mph (240 kph)

Z more than 149 mph (over 240 kph)

Next, you will want the right price and tire size for your vehicle. If you look on the sidewall or in the brochure, you will notice a string of numbers and letters.

Tire size P205/70R14H

The P indicates that it is for a passenger vehicle. The number 205 is the width of the tire measured in millimeters. Usually the wider the tire, the better traction and handling a vehicle will have, but check ahead to find out what size will fit on your car as each car has its size limitations. The number 70 indicates the ratio of the height to the width. Here, the lower the number (percentage) is for tires, the better traction and handling, as they lower the car and its center of gravity. The R tells you that it is a radial type tire, D is for bias ply and B indicates that they are bias belted. Remember not to mix the different types. The number 14 is the diameter of the rim; it is important to buy the right size of tire, since you can't fit a 14 inch tire on a 15 inch rim. The letter H represents the speed rating (see above). Some tires have an additional number after the rim size (eg. P205/70R1482H). The 82 is the load index and will tell you the maximum load allowable for this tire.

There have been some questions raised in the past about using solid rubber tires. People felt that they would last longer than those used today (and therefore hurt the rubber industry). Others thought that such tires would reduce drag and road friction and therefore increase road mileage. Introducing solid rubber tires would require some drastic alterations to a vehicle's suspension and other systems. Maybe with enough research and development, companies can introduce a solid rubber or other material tire that has a longer life-span than the ones we have now and is also more environmentally-friendly.

Auto Body Shop

Before choosing an auto body shop it is important to decide what type, quality and price range of work you are looking for. Unlike many other automobile repairs, most body work, other than serious collisions, are done for cosmetic reasons. The safety and reliability of the car are not affected by the quality of a paint job or the removal of rust and dents. This leaves more room for decisions that can't be made when fixing brakes: the quality of body work is much easier for someone to judge and there is usually no urgency to these repairs. One can drive around getting estimates and advice from shops for months before making a decision.

Many shops will specialize in different areas and styles of work, not only focusing on different types of repairs, but also different qualities of work on the same repair. For example, one shop may pride itself in doing a paint job everyone will stop and stare at; to them painting a car is a work of art. This type of shop will likely take great care and attention, but the price will also be very high. To find a shop like this, when you see a car with a beautiful paint job, ask the owner where it was done.

Another shop prides itself in being able to do a fast and passable paint job for a cheaper price than most others. Shops like this often advertise heavily and offer coupons. The paint job here will look nothing like the art of the previously mentioned shop, but will be a fraction of the price. You have a better chance of getting what you want, at the best price, when you are at a shop that focuses on what you are looking for. This applies to all types of auto body repairs. Just because a shop is great at painting does not mean it can properly straighten out the car frame after a bad accident. These areas require completely different skills and equipment.

The type of work you want done on your car depends on the type of car, its importance to you and how good you want it to look. If you regard your car as cheap transportation, you will likely want cheap but passable work done. This assumes that the work will have no effect on the safety of the car. If you have a beautiful collector car, you may wish to have the best, lasting work done, and increase the value of the car even further. Once you have decided what quality of work you want, you should be able to clearly distinguish between top quality and run-of-the-mill workmanship.

One of the best distinguishing factors between high and poor quality work is how the shop deals with **rust**. A good job would entail sanding or cutting out all of the rust right down to the bare metal before applying paint. A poor job would be simply smoothing out and then covering over the rust so that you don't see it is there until it breaks through the new paint. Regardless of what quality of paint job you are looking for, it is always a good idea to eliminate all rust before painting.

Try to get a written guarantee that rust won't reappear in the same spot for a lengthy period of time to ensure that they don't just paint over it. Many shops will not want to give this type of guarantee, but it is worth a try.

If you have a valuable car with a small but serious rust problem, you probably want a **cut and weld job**. This is the old-fashioned way of doing things and it will be harder to find a good shop. This involves cutting out the rust and welding in a new piece of metal. It requires lots of skill and work and not just anyone can do it. Try to get someone who specializes in this. Look for good references and shop around.

For a quicker and less expensive repair of a rust hole, many shops will use **fiberglass filler** to covers the rust hole. This can be quite effective as long as the rust around the area is completely removed. This is not a big problem for a shop to do if they want to, and if you make them feel they will not get away with less than a thorough job. Sandblasting the area can clean things up quite nicely.

If your car begins to rust, buy a can of rust remover and polish away the little rust spots when they first appear. This will help prevent the rust from further damaging your car. Wash your car regularly, especially if you live in an area where the air is salty or spread on the street in icy weather. Don't forget to spray the underside of the car with water to remove salt which will eat away the metal.

If the rust on part of your car is already out of control you have several options (if the car is structurally sound and not ready to fall apart or rust out completely). The trick is to get quotes on restoring the damaged part in comparison to purchasing a new or used part. For example, if you have a badly rusted (or even dented) door, it may be cheaper to get a used door from a scrap dealer. Then you can have a body shop touch it up, paint it to match and install it on your car, rather than fixing the gaping rust holes and dents on the one you already have. Body shops will often undertake this kind of work. It is advisable to first track down the part on your own by calling scrap dealers, telling them your car model and make and the part you want. Once you have found the part, get a price for the replacement and body work. This prevents the body shop from overcharging you, by trying to make a profit on the new part. This option can save money, but is a lot of work and not for everyone.

Chrome parts of the car can be repaired if damaged by surface rust. Special metal plating shops will re-chrome automotive parts. This process is not cheap, but is less expensive in most cases than purchasing a new part.

When getting **paint** work done, make it clear to the shop beforehand that you will not tolerate poorly-matched paint. Nothing looks worse than a car with different colors of paint on a door or some other panel. Paint matching can take time even for a skilled painter because of the natural fading and changes in a car's paint over time. Stressing the importance of this can result in that extra effort to get things right the first time, saving problems later.

Many shops say they will repair or paint a large part of the car, when in reality these shops paint where they feel it is necessary and tape over the rest. When the paint dries, they polish what they should have painted so that you can't tell the difference and you are overcharged for the amount of work done.

Ask to see the car, when it is primed (sanded and base coat applied) before painting. If a lot of rust is being removed, ask to see the car just after it is sanded so that you can inspect the metal for any rust still present.

Serious collision repairs should be covered by auto insurance, and therefore your number one concern is to get the best job possible by choosing the most competent shop (however, with ever increasing insurance premiums, we should all try not to abuse the system.)

When choosing a shop, take a look at some cars waiting to be picked up and check to see that the paint matches and quality work has been done. A good sign is when there are lots of nice cars in the shop and not only beaters. Make sure the cars are kept in a safe, uncluttered and orderly area to prevent additional bumps and scrapes before and after the work is done.

Once someone brought his car in for some work and when he picked it up, discovered his radio knobs missing and a big scratch on the passenger side door. They were both fixed only because he checked the car carefully before paying the bill. Believe it or not, this all happened at a luxury car dealership. It is also a good idea to make a note of your odometer reading to be sure no one takes your car on a trip over the weekend. Check for any grease stains left on the interior by a careless mechanic.

Check your car over carefully, both inside and out, after any repair, *before* paying the bill. Once the bill is paid, you surrender most of the power you posses to resolve any problems there may be. Don't just check what was supposed to be done, check everything. Once you pay the check and leave you are probably out of luck.

114

When it comes to having a collision repair done, one distinction is important to understand. There are two body types on cars. Older cars have **heavy steel frames** with everything attached to them, allowing for more basic repair techniques. However, most cars these days are made with **unibody construction**. This means that each piece of the car's shell fits together perfectly to make one unit. The problem is, after an accident, it is often hard to tell what parts are out of alignment. Expensive equipment is required to find and properly fix the problem. Without this high-tech equipment, the job will be poorly done. This means that even though the car may look great after repair, it may be unstable and unsafe to drive.

Even the welding process for unibody cars (called "MIG welding") must be done with a special welder (not something every shop has) or the metal may be ruined. Furthermore, special training is required for the mechanic to properly operate all this equipment and to correctly do the repairs. When you have had a unibody repair done, and suddenly find the alignment is off, have the problem looked at right away in the interest of safety to make sure the repair was done correctly. If you have a hard time talking to the shop, enlist the help of the insurance agency to make things move along more smoothly.

Minor body work is one area in which, regardless of experience, anyone may learn and attempt the work themselves. Good results can often be achieved, with no danger to others, other than an eyesore. The basic things needed to do simple repairs may be purchased from automotive supply shops for reasonable prices. There are tons of books available on body repairs that explain what damage you will be able to repair and how to do it. With patience, hard work and effort, it is possible to do a decent repair job. Some people find this type of work both relaxing and rewarding. Removing minor rust, or fixing a small hole can cost only a few dollars when done yourself in comparison to hundreds when done by a shop.

On the other hand, if you want it done professionally or the repair is beyond your ability or interest, there are many shops out there that can do the work.

A combination of doing the preparatory work yourself and having the final prep and paint job done professionally can lead to better results than if the shop does the whole thing. You may take more care in removing all the rust from your car, plus filling and sanding minor blemishes, because it's your car, whereas the shop has hundreds of cars to think about. In addition, this type of work is time consuming no matter who does it, and it will often save you money if you do it before bringing the car into the shop.

Above all, find the right shop for the particular job at hand. The customer who thinks he should come first is already at a huge disadvantage when showing up at a shop with work in which they don't specialize. Not only does the shop not care if you walk right out the door taking your business elsewhere, they will likely quote you a high price. In addition, the shop will likely not do that great of a job, due to lack of the necessary skill, equipment or enthusiasm.

For example, Tony needs to get a bad rust hole in the side of his door cut out and a new piece of metal welded in. He takes his problem to a big high-tech shop that specializes in unibody repairs and deals almost exclusively with insurance company claims: strike one against Tony. The shop manager then thinks, "I don't want my technician pulled away from his usual job to play around with a delicate welding job he may have to do three times to get right. Look at the money the shop will lose:" strike two.

Finally, the shop manager figures he will send it to a shop that specializes in this type of repair. To make it worth while, the price must go up so everyone makes a profit: strike three. If poor Tony gets the work done here, he will not only be treated like a second class citizen, he will overpay for the job, and possibly have poor follow-up service if there is a problem. Tony would be better off finding a few shops that specialize in cut and weld jobs who would appreciate his business. Here he could negotiate the best price and deal directly with the shop doing the work.

Much of the initial investigation can be done over the phone. In the phone book, many auto body shops will list what type of repairs they specialize in. Call around first and narrow your list down to the shops who seem interested in your particular problem and then compare these.

If at all possible, try not to let a tow truck driver take you to the body or repair shop of his choice after an accident or mechanical problem. Often kickbacks are given to the tow truck driver bringing business to a particular shop. This is a bad way to start off, especially when a serious repair is needed. It is better to keep a list of shops you have either heard good things about or used previously in the glove box for such situations. You can then call ahead from a phone booth and control where you go, rather than just walking into a trap.

Towing

Your vehicle may break down while on the road for one reason or another, possibly as a result of an automobile accident. Of course, the chances of having a breakdown due to a lack of proper maintenance are slim now that you have read the information in this book. If you are reading this chapter and are not yet confident about your vehicle's status, then either read the appropriate chapter or check in the maintenance section to verify that everything has been done.

You should know what your owner's manual says about having your vehicle towed. Some vehicles have specific information regarding safe towing. Serious damage can result from ignoring these points and may end up costing you a significant sum of money for additional repairs. When trouble does occur, the tow truck driver may not be aware of the small details pertaining to your vehicle, so have that information ready for him. Some cars, for example, have a bumper system that will not allow towing. If it is ever towed by the bumper, serious damage will result. Tow truck operators will usually shrug it off and say they know what to do, but inform them politely anyhow and watch them carefully as they hook your vehicle up.

Tow trucks come in a four basic varieties. One type uses **chains and cables** to hook up the bumpers. These are rarely seen in cities anymore, but you may find them operating in less populated regions. If the operator is not careful with the chains, they can damage a vehicle's suspension system and bumper. There is also a danger if the vehicle is a newer model. They are equipped with bumpers designed to absorb some of the crushing force in an accident, so that upon the initial impact certain sections will collapse and most of the force will be dissipated before reaching you. You can imagine what can happen to this sensitive bumper if the total weight of your vehicle is suspended from it by a long chain at the back of a tow truck. This is quite different from the older vehicles around. In the 60s and 70s, companies like Ford and General Motors used to make cars with bumpers that were part of the frame. These cars could almost ram through brick walls.

A more common type of tow truck uses a **frame device** that, when clamped together, will lift your vehicle by its wheels. As your car was designed to bear weight on its wheels, you can see how this system is much better and safer.

A word of caution though; when your car is being towed from the front make sure that the wheels are straight. If they are turned, your car's wheel alignment may be affected.

A friend's car was towed with the front wheels turned because the tow truck operator did not position his truck properly. As a consequence, the next day the car began to wander off to the right while driving. The wheel alignment had been affected. Your case may not be as severe, but the friend was forced to shell out extra money to repair his car. This type of damage is difficult to blame on the towing company. Prevent it before it happens.

Other types of trucks use the traditional **hook and chains**. As these are attached to the undercarriage of your car, where many parts lie, certain damage may result. The chains may affect vital brake or fuel lines, steering joints or even plastic pieces located in the front or rear of the vehicle. If a brake line is twisted, a problem may not be detected until a much later date when the driver is in danger of having brake failure. Windshield damage has also occurred due to an inexperienced operator, so watch the operator as he hooks up your vehicle.

A last option is a **flat-bed truck**. These are large trucks with a long platform in the rear. Your car can safely be pulled on using a powered winch and then locked in with chains to secure it. There it will rest, as if parked, while traveling to the garage or driveway. These types of trucks are used when an automobile has sustained severe damage to the wheels (usually from an auto-accident) that makes it untowable. You can also request one as the need arises. There may be a greater service fee for this type of truck, so inquire first. Even at a greater expense, it may be worth it.

Some Automobile Associations make a towing service available to members. Other towing companies may also be affiliated with these associations, but you can usually expect a qualified driver in either case.

If you don't have a membership at present, you may wish to join, since towing done through the association is free. In addition, for a low yearly membership fee you will gain access to emergency roadside assistance and travel information, among other service benefits.

In the case of a driving accident, don't allow your vehicle to be towed until all information is taken with the police present (note: in some cities, police no longer attend unless it is an injury-accident). This will include a report of sustained damage to you, your vehicle and on-site witnesses. Be very careful if anyone asks you to sign an authorization form to do estimates on the damage. They could charge for this service. Get the insurance company to either select an estimator or send one to the shop the car will be sent to.

When your vehicle is towed while illegally parked, contact the towing company right away. Theft and vandalism can occur to cars stored at the towing yard for too long. When you pick up your car, check it over to ensure that there is no new damage, missing parts or valuables.

It is often difficult for people to check their car properly because they are too angry that their precious car was towed or at the inconvenience and expense it has caused them. Don't let this blind you. The more rational you are, the better chance of noticing something wrong with your vehicle. If you do find something new, report it to the front desk and put it in writing on the bill. Later, you can obtain repair estimates and pictures and approach the towing company with your complaint. At that point they could either comply or completely deny any allegations. That bill then becomes important if you decide to file suit against them.

Automotive Security

Automotive security has boomed into an industry of its own in recent years. The market has been flooded with high-tech alarm systems with all sorts of options. A few visits to stores that specialize in this equipment will dazzle you. **Alarms** range from basic ones that will sound when the doors are opened, to talking alarms that will tell someone when they are standing too close to the car. The price range of these alarms will vary as much as their functions. Many alarm systems now have motion detectors and contacts that will sound the alarm when any area of the car is tampered with. If you show interest in spending money in a specialty shop, more options than you could dream up in a science fiction movie will pass your eyes.

The problem with alarms is that people have become used to hearing them. There are so many false alarms that people are desensitized to them, and do not automatically equate a sounding alarm with a car being stolen. This means that if you are not within hearing distance of the car alarm and familiar with its sound, it may do little good, especially with car thieves becoming so adept at deactivating alarm systems. To combat this problem, many car alarms now come equipped with **pagers**. These will beep or vibrate to let the car owner know that someone has bumped into, broken into or is stealing their car.

This sounds great in theory, but in practice, does the average car owner want to risk his or her life catching and confronting someone who may be armed and dangerous, just to save their car and some money? The value of an alarm depends on your ability to react to it. In a recent case in a West Coast city, a good Samaritan caught two thieves breaking into a strip of cars downtown. The Samaritan tried to stop them single-handedly and was stabbed to death for his efforts. In some cases, it may be wiser to call the police and let them handle the situation.

An alarm system could be useful when someone parks their car near their apartment or house every night. If a thief sets off the alarm, you can yell out the window and call the police. If you are worried about your car being stolen while at a movie or shopping, it may be much less effective as no one may respond to the alarm.

Many alarm systems now come equipped with a **kill switch**. The kill switch is installed somewhere inside the car, known only to the driver. The switch can be turned on to prevent the car from being driven by anyone who does not know its location. There are other variations on this idea, but basically they just make it that much harder for someone to steal your car. With the number of cars out there without protection, most criminals don't want to bother with alarm equipment. They can find many cars without it. In fact, a surprisingly high number of cars stolen were unlocked and many even had the keys in the ignition. With vehicles like these around, alarm systems definitely do reduce the chance of a car being stolen.

A great theft deterrent are the new high quality **steering wheel locks**. These are less expensive than electronic alarms and are visible to a criminal. These are metal bars that lock onto the steering wheel and prevent it from turning without smashing the front window or steering column. It is important to get a steering wheel lock of high quality so that it can not be easily dismantled by a criminal. If you have one, you should use it every time you leave your car. Many thefts happen when one least expects it, and often very quickly. The disadvantage is they only prevent someone from stealing the car, but not from tampering with or vandalizing it.

You should always keep a spare key for the steering wheel lock in a safe place. It can be quite expensive to have one of these devices removed from your car without the key.

The combination of a steering wheel lock and a basic alarm system can make your car an unattractive target to most criminals. If a true pro really wants your car, there isn't much you can do to stop him, however, the odds are greatly reduced that anyone will bother to try.

Another inexpensive trick is to have serial numbers etched into the glass on all the windows of your car.

This will further make your car less attractive to thieves, because not only does it increase their chances of being caught, but it reduces chop shop or resale value due to the ruined auto glass.

Another good tip is to drop a recent business card with the current date down the door or in some other hard to reach spot. If your car gets stolen and the serial numbers are changed, you have additional proof that the car was yours.

This brings us to the next issue of people trying to steal what is either inside the car or attached to it. It is never a good idea to leave valuables, or anything that can be perceived as valuable, lying around inside of the car. This will attract thieves. When a criminal tries to break into a car to steal something inside, much more damage is done to the vehicle than simply the loss of the item. Windows may be broken, seats torn and all sorts of other nasty things. For some reason, many criminals can't stop at stealing, but also feel a need to vandalize the inside of the victim's car.

Another common crime problem is the theft of car stereo systems. When one has a valuable stereo in the car it greatly increases the chance of having a problem. Many thieves focus on stealing them, literally looking from car to car until a stereo catches their eye. Often even the best alarm systems will not stop these characters, because they will simply smash the car window, let the alarm sound, pull out the stereo and run away. For this reason, many car stereos are now equipped with pull out features that allow the owner to remove either the whole stereo or the face plate when leaving the car. Special face plates are now available that give fancy stereos a cheap look. This is a good deterrent product. Some drivers choose to attach things like extra amplifiers or equalizers to the floor of the car and simply cover them up when leaving.

Vandalism is another big problem. Alarm companies have capitalized on this by making ultra sensitive alarm systems to detect this sort of invasion. For example, some alarms can even be hooked up to the hood ornaments of fancier cars. However, one must be realistic; if some kid breaks off the hood ornament from a Cedilla for his collection, will the alarm sounding stop him, and make him put it back? At most, the delinquent will run away faster than he normally would have.

One of the greatest fears in car security is the theft of mint condition older cars, which have a low replacement value from any insurance company when stolen.

Get a written appraisal of your car to better show your car's value if necessary (this is also valuable if the car is ever written off in a bad accident). Be sure to get your car in top shape before the appraisal, save repair receipts and take pictures. Many of these older cars have door lock buttons with the little knob on top. These door locks are susceptible to break-ins by amateurs using a coat hanger. It is a good idea to change these door locks to the ones that are smooth with no edges.

A common problem when parking your car is that someone will scratch or chip the paint. Usually this happens either on purpose by someone with a sharp object or by accident when someone parked too close to you opens their door.

When a scratch or chip like this occurs, fill it in immediately with some touch-up paint if it's not very serious and you do not intend to get a full repair done right away. Small tubes of touch-up paint can be bought at most auto supply stores at a nominal cost. This will prevent a small scratch from turning into a larger rust problem. Any exposed metal will rust quickly and can end up being much more expensive to repair.

When it comes to purchasing an alarm system, advice is hard to give because they are changing every day. There is no question that both a steering wheel lock and an alarm system will lessen the chances of having a problem. Shop around and ask lots of questions. How easy is it for a thief to disarm the system? Does this alarm automatically stall the car if someone tries to steal it? Is the installation included in the price? What is the warranty? What do I do if this alarm malfunctions and I can't turn it off? How much strain does this system put on my battery? Can this system be upgraded if I choose to later on? Overall, security needs and choices will be different depending on the type of car, area you park in, personal preferences and the amount of money you want to spend.

Conclusion

We all depend a great deal on our vehicles for our livelihood, placing great demands upon them which can add up and take their toll. Without proper maintenance, a car simply won't last that long, and if it does stay around for 10 years, the later maintenance and repair costs will be horrendous. Cars can last indefinitely if carefully looked after. If you want proof, just go to one of those antique car shows. You don't have to go to that extent or expense, but doesn't that show you how durable these vehicles can be?

Learn as much as you can about your particular vehicle. If your schedule allows it, take a course on basic car repair and maintenance. Women should also not feel intimidated when it comes to car care. Probably the most effective way to learn is to take an introductory course, or get a friend to teach you some basics. Another good source of basic information, and one which many people forget, is the owner's manual. This manual gives details concerning your specific vehicle and is simple enough to understand for the average car owner.

Be calm in the face of repairs and don't look for a super cheap job; it may be really "cheap," but it may not be that "super." Look for a fair price on competent work. Keep in mind that automotive mechanics are human and are entitled to make mistakes. So, before getting angry with them, analyze the situation and act accordingly. If you are dissatisfied with their quote, you then have the option to leave and find a mechanic elsewhere. Regarding repairs, you will have to point out details of their failing to satisfy you (poorly-done repairs, unnecessary repairs, work not done, etc.) and from there you will be able to come to a middle ground on the final bill. When your repair bills are consistently high and you are not driving a Mercedes or equivalent, the problem may also be a poorly constructed vehicle and the best solution could be to trade it in for a better car.

Refer back to specific chapters of this book as you need them. A quick review before going in for a repair can save you alot of money and be well worth the time. This book is meant to make owning a car more of an enjoyable experience and less of a nightmare. Since it doesn't require that much time to figure out what your car needs, it is going to be well worth your time to understand it a little. The next time you go into a shop you won't feel like you're paying for the mechanic's next vacation and who knows, maybe with the money you save you can take a holiday yourself!

Good luck!

Mario Sasso

Michael Ross